BLAME IT ON THE DOG

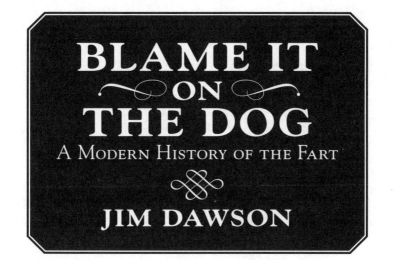

BLAME IT ON THE DOG

A MODERN HISTORY OF THE FART

JIM DAWSON

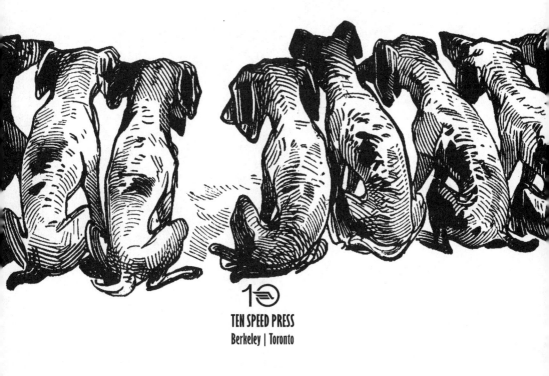

TEN SPEED PRESS
Berkeley | Toronto

1🖉⊃

Ten Speed Press
PO Box 7123
Berkeley, California 94707
www.tenspeed.com

Distributed in Australia by Simon & Schuster Australia, in Canada by Ten Speed Press
Canada, in New Zealand by Southern Publishers Group, in South Africa by Real Books,
and in the United Kingdom and Europe by Publishers Group UK.

Cover design by Betsy Stromberg
Text design by Chris Hall

Library of Congress Cataloging-in-Publication Data
Dawson, Jim.
Blame it on the dog : a modern history of the fart / Jim Dawson.
   p. cm.
Includes index.
ISBN-13: 978-1-58008-751-3
ISBN-10: 1-58008-751-5
   1. Flatulence—Humor. I. Title.
PN6231.F55D39 2006
818'.602—dc22

                    2006011433
First printing, 2006
Printed in the United States of America

1 2 3 4 5 6 7 8 9 10 — 10 09 08 07 06

CONTENTS

INTRODUCTION

"A fart is just a turd with all the shit scraped off," a sage told me several years ago, implying that flatulence wasn't a subject worthy of filling a book—or at least a book worth a hill of beans. But what did he know? The idea of writing the definitive history of farting had been nagging at me for thirty years, since my student days and wayward nights at West Virginia University, a notorious party school. It wasn't the all-night keggers and marijuana binges that inspired me (though they certainly helped), but rather the English literature class where I discovered the fart jokes in Chaucer's fourteenth-century *Canterbury Tales.* And by 1998, when the time—like a good fart—seemed ripe, I approached Ten Speed Press with a coffee-stained, thumb-smudged, and altogether unsavory-looking manuscript called *Who Cut the Cheese? A Cultural History of the Fart.* (All right, it was actually an email attachment, but a mysteriously soiled manuscript sounds much more romantic; and if nothing else, this sordid saga of a grown man obsessing on butt stink could use some romance.)

The rest is history, and that's probably where it belongs, but I've never been one to leave well enough alone. After all, I'm still psychologically smarting from the humiliation of being tarred, feathered, and run out of my home town of Parkersburg, West Virginia, for hosting an art gallery exhibit of X-rays of my lower colon, with superimposed green arrows pointing out that the little gray blobby areas were farts about to happen.

On the eve of the publication of *Who Cut the Cheese?* my editor solemnly sat me down and told me, "Jim, when this thing comes out, your life is going to change. I mean *really* change. People will revile you, call you a sick bastard. Pretty women will shun you like the plague."

"I know all *that*," I said, "but how is my life gonna change?"

(Actually, several attractive women did stop me on the street after the publication of *Who Cut the Cheese?* They asked me questions like "Why are you following me?")

Anyway, when the book came out at the beginning of February 1999, none of the major magazines or newspapers would touch it. A columnist I knew at the *Los Angeles Times* told me that no family newspaper would dare print the word *fart*. But fortunately there was one corner of the media that greeted me with open arms: morning drive–time radio, where shock jocks and wacky zoo triplets were waiting for an excuse to air the second F word (the FCC having expressly prohibited the first) and discuss its many facets. For six or seven months I was up almost every weekday morning around 4:00 or 5:00 A.M., Los Angeles time, standing in my kitchen in my underwear or sweatpants, pumping coffee down my throat in hopes of ratcheting up my ability to engage with motormouth deejays in the eastern time zones without falling back on a slight stutter I've had since childhood. Being a night owl who normally didn't get to bed before 2:00 A.M., I had a tough time with this schedule and stumbled around in a perpetual state of jet lag, yet still I pursued my new mission as America's emissary of toilet humor with doo-doo diligence.

I think I did a phoner with every A.M. radio program in America except Howard Stern's. (Howard's staff pre-interviewed me, and Howard talked about *Who Cut the Cheese?* on the air, remarking pointedly that no way could a book about farts be as funny as the real thing, but I never got to speak to him personally.) First I'd get a call from the producer, who would give me a last-minute prep, put me on hold, and let me listen to the commercials and the bumper music on the feed until the on-air personalities introduced me to the audience and punched me into the show. I couldn't help but notice the similarities between them, whether they were in Birmingham, New York, or Birmingham, Alabama. Most of the jocks came in threes, with monikers like Frosty, Tammi, and the Bean, and approached me one of two ways: I was either this cool guy who had come up with the greatest book idea ever (the "I'm too sexy for my farts" Jim) or some creep who'd crawled out from under a rock (the "Yes, I really do stink!" Jim). I would figure out which one they were looking for—cool or creepy—and play along. During one phone-in, the girl of the team dramatically evacuated herself from the studio before my voice came on. But who cared, as long as listeners bought my book.

As it turned out, many people did. The book has sold many tens of thousands of copies, has gone into its tenth printing, and continues to sell at a steady pace seven years later. Two other books called *Who Cut the Cheese?* (with different subtitles) came out a year or so after mine. They were both parodies of Dr. Spencer Johnson's best seller, *Who Moved My Cheese?* In England, where I'd done several phoners and appeared on a BBC radio special, Michael O'Mara Books, a publisher of novelties and knockoffs, commandeered the clever cover art from *Who Cut the Cheese?* and printed a somewhat faded facsimile on two of its own paperbacks, including *The Little Book of Farting.* The cover, a detail of *Thirty-Six Faces of Expression* by Louis Boilly, had been painted in France some 150 years earlier, so nobody was in a position to sue. Besides, isn't imitation a sincere form of flatulence?

Since I had become the national crepitation clearinghouse, not to mention the only American who could bet that the words "who cut the cheese?" would be in the first sentence of his obituary, many radio callers and letter writers were anxious to give me new material or correct some of my information. For example, I had written about the "blue dart"—the methane flame-up you get when you light a fart—without mentioning "blue angel," the term most popular in Canada and England. Someone else added to my list of flatulent food items by informing me that the then-popular diet drug Fen-Phen would make you fart-phart. A Latin scholar chastised me for mistranslating *crepitus ventris* as a "crackling wind." I had made *crepitus* an adjective, he said, when in fact it's a noun, and *ventris* has nothing to do with wind—it's the genitive singular of *venter* (belly, stomach)—so the phrase means "a crackling or rumbling of the stomach." "Crackling wind in Latin would be *crepitans ventus,*" he scolded with the finger-wagging authority of an Oxford don.

In addition, new fart factoids kept arriving every week from magazines, newspapers, the Internet, and enlightened friends and acquaintances. After a while, all that stuff just piled up, and like a big gas bubble in the lower intestine, it had only one place to go: in this case, a sequel to *Who Cut the Cheese?* featuring sound bites (a term rather suspicious in this context) from the past several years.

There were some serious discussions about what to call the new book. Somebody suggested the clever *Son of Who Cut the Cheese.* I lobbied for a title that broke the (cheese) mold: *Farts and the Men Who Let Them.* But my editor said, "That's a kicker, not a title," which means we would have ended up with something like *Butt Blasts! Farts and the Men Who Let Them.* Ultimately, it was decided that men really didn't need any extra encouragement to express their masculinity by pushing blunt air through their anuses. In that case, I suggested, shouldn't we call it *All Right, Guys, Let's Cut the Ma-cheeze-mo?*

Well, nobody likes a smart-ass. Especially a farting one.

Then someone (a guilt-ridden pet owner, no doubt) suggested I pay homage to our four-legged best friends, who loyally and silently bear our human shame whenever we're too cowardly to take responsibility ourselves. Voilà! There was our title.

But then, just a few days later, I saw a news item about an Iowa company, Flat-D Inventions, that's marketing an antifart thong for canines called the Dogone (www.flat-d.com/canineproducts.html). It's basically an activated-charcoal strip—the company refers to it as a Dog Gas Neutralizing Pad—that straps over the canine's ass, with a hole for the tail to stick through. The Dogone comes in large (Saint Bernards), medium (spaniels), and small (Pomeranians). When I contacted owner Frank Morosky, he told me, "The unfortunate thing about the product is that you cannot blame it on the dog anymore." What's he trying to do, kill my book before it's even off the press?

We cannot know what the future holds for canine flatulence odor control products, but for now, I hope you enjoy *Blame It on the Dog.*

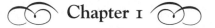

Chapter 1

THE POWERFUL LITTLE FART:
A REFRESHER

Since this is a book about flatulence, I should probably begin by going back over a few of the basics. After all, some of you may have never noticed those little hot bubbles coming out of your butt, and maybe you've misidentified the noises as chair squeaks, mice in the walls, or the family dog. Sorry to inform you, but you fart just like everyone else. Sure, you were born with a sterile gut, but it didn't take you long to pick up a few intestinal bacteria and join the human family of farters. A guy with a healthy diet lets out about a quart of gas every day, broken up into anywhere from ten to fifteen farts of various magnitudes; women fart slightly less, maybe only eight or nine times a day, but their gas is more concentrated. Still, many women will tell you they never fart at all, or if they do, their dainty poofs have only a slight fragrance, pleasant to the nose. It's probably best if you just agree with them.

Flatulence, or intestinal gas, is composed of roughly three-fifths nitrogen, one-fifth hydrogen, one-tenth carbon dioxide, and small amounts of methane and oxygen—all of which are essentially odorless. What creates the unpleasantness are trace amounts of other chemicals, especially ammonia, hydrogen sulfide, and skatole (from the Greek *skatos*, meaning excrement), that stink so pungently, people can smell them at levels of 1 part per 100 million parts of air. The human colon—according to Dr. Paul Eckburg, Stanford University

DNA researcher—has at least 395 different types of bacteria, but *E. coli* is the main culprit, creating gas by munching away at that meal you ate a few hours ago and then microfarting what it doesn't need. The nitrogen comes from blood diffusion through the stomach walls, and the oxygen is mostly swallowed air. Indeed, dogs are very flatulent—and easy to blame your farts on—because they gulp lots of air as they're lapping up their food and water.

Beans, mushrooms, cabbages, and onions are among the main gas-producing foods because they contain complex sugars that your body simply can't break down. These sugars ferment inside you like grapes in a wine vat, the only difference being that there's never a good year for farts.

Your flatus (that's the Latin word) initially has a temperature of 98.6°F, just like you, but it cools quickly as it flies away from "ground zero" at ten feet per second. If someone is standing nearby, your fart finds him like a heat-seeking missile and goes right up his nose, where millions of receptor cells in the mucous lining transform the molecules into electrical signals and send them along through nerve fibers right into his brain. If you've ever thought *I'd sure like to get inside that guy's head,* well, now you know how to do it.

Along with *le persistance* (the lingering effect), a fart has what French perfumers call *sillage*—the wake that follows you, whispering "*j'accuse*" as you leave the room. The only way to stop it from stalking you is to inconspicuously drop your hand behind your back and wave it back and forth with a gentle wrist motion. In English, this is called "breaking the trail," though I'm sure the French have a fancier term for it. If your fart has lots of *persistance* and plenty of *sillage*, it's the next best thing to being in several places at once, for even after you've gone, everyone else will swear you're still there.

It's never much fun catching a whiff or a blast of somebody else's fart, but believe it or not, there's an upside. According to an early 2004 item in *Science Daily,* Dr. Richard Doty at the University of Pennsylvania School of Medicine found that one of the first things to go as people get Alzheimer's, Parkinson's, and other neurodegenerative diseases is the sense of smell. In fact, he and other researchers are hoping to devise a smell test to detect early clinical signs of these maladies. So take heart every time you're suddenly overwhelmed by someone's anal fumes. You might feel like you're losing consciousness, but at least you're not losing your mind.

So there you have it in a nutshell: the fart, your funny little friend. Now let's get to the good stuff.

Chapter 2

A BEER FART (ALMOST) HEARD ROUND THE WORLD

On Super Bowl Sunday, ninety million people all over the world tune in to television's most overhyped event, not simply to watch professional football's championship game, but also to see what clever advertising Madison Avenue has dreamed up for this special day. Spectacular commercials have been a tradition at Super Bowls since 1984, when Apple, announcing its new personal Macintosh computer, set the bar high for eye-catching creativity with a $1.6 million Orwellian production by *Blade Runner* director Ridley Scott. By February 1, 2004, twenty years later, ad rates for the Super Bowl had risen to $2 million a minute. With that kind of money, advertisers needed a lot of bang for the buck.

One of the commercials that CBS ran that day was a Bud Light beer moment called "Sleigh Ride," based loosely on a 1996 *Seinfeld* TV episode called "The Rye," in which a flatulent horse, pulling one of New York's famous Central Park carriages, unleashed an unholy wind upon several unsuspecting passengers. (The episode, incidentally, was written by a woman—comedian Carol Leifer—so let's hear none of that stuff about just guys farting around.) In "Sleigh Ride," a young man is taking his girlfriend on a romantic horse-drawn spin around the park. Hoping to celebrate a treasured harmony of two hearts beating as one, he lights a candle, hands it to his beloved, and, bending down to reach into a cooler of cold Bud Lights, says, "We need something to make this moment really wonderful." The horse takes this opportunity to lift its tail and rip a silent-but-deadly Clydesdale-worthy fart directly into the girl's face. When our hero raises back up with the two cans of beer, his girlfriend is still holding the now-smoldering candle, but her eyes are dazed and her hair and eyebrows have been singed by the methane flare.

According to instant polls by *USA Today*, America Online (AOL), and the ad agency website ADBOWL (http://adbowl.com), "Sleigh Ride" ranked among the most popular commercials aired during the game. Yet "Sleigh Ride" was almost forgotten in the aftermath of the halftime show, during which alleged singer Justin Timberlake yanked on R&B superstar Janet Jackson's breakaway bustier and exposed her right boob (though her nipple remained hidden under a pasty) for a second or two, bringing the world to the type of sudden standstill that would follow a loud fart at a presidential funeral. The twenty-four-hour cable news networks were shocked, *shocked* that such a thing could happen during the only television program that routinely attracts viewers from every demographic—from apple-cheeked kids to kindly grandmothers—which may account for why they indignantly reran the boob flash several dozen times an hour for the next two weeks straight. Outraged Federal Communications Commission (FCC) chairman Michael Powell denounced the incident as "classless, crass, and deplorable," and slapped a $550,000 fine on CBS, the largest ever imposed for indecency. If that weren't bad enough, the stunt spurred a media outcry against all the smut and degeneracy that had been creeping into TV and radio over the past two decades. Clear Channel Communications, a powerful media conglomerate of over 1,200 radio stations, ordered the cancellation of several morning shock jocks, including Bubba the Love Sponge and Howard Stern. By March 8, the FCC said it had received 530,828 complaints about Ms. Jackson's breast (and apparently none about the equine beer fart)—though most of them came from email mills like the Parents Television Council in Los Angeles. (Perhaps H. L. Mencken's word for the general American public, "booboisie," would apply here.) Under pressure from angry conservatives, Congress passed new regulations upping FCC fines tenfold, from $32,500 per incident to $350,000. To escape any further *fartwas* from the FCC ayatollahs, Howard Stern eventually bolted for Sirius Radio, a subscription satellite operation that broadcasts beyond the agency's bailiwick. Ultimately, the government's response to the hooter hullabaloo chilled free speech and instituted the policy of "When in doubt, leave it out"—not the best idea in a democracy that depends on open discussion.

Behind all this postgame hysteria is the FCC's ambiguous definition of indecency, defined as "language or material that, in context, depicts or describes, in terms patently offensive as measured by contemporary community standards for the broadcast medium, sexual or excretory organs or activities." Though indecency by that standard applies equally to tits and farts, the FCC determined that a semi-bare breast in *your* face is more indecent than a horse fart in some poor girl's face. Maybe it had something to do with the fact that the commission is overseen by the House Committee on Energy and Commerce, known for its cozy relationship with gas industry lobbyists. Or maybe it's because Americans are more frightened of sex than anal eruptions. In any event, fart lovers should be thankful that Janet Jackson flashed her mam instead of baring her right gluteus and ripping off a flatus maximus at the audience.

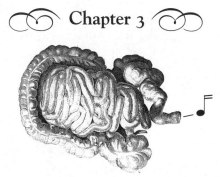

Chapter 3

THE MAN WITH THE SINGING SPHINCTER!

The chapter in *Who Cut the Cheese?* that got the most reaction from readers was the story of Joseph Pujol, better known as Le Petomane, whose amazing rectum could sing and mimic an assortment of sounds, including, he claimed, the voice of his mother-in-law. In the early 1890s, his farting displays at the Moulin Rouge in Paris brought in more customers than even the soliloquies of the great actress Sarah Bernhardt. But Le Petomane's act was apparently never filmed or recorded, an oversight that left a void in Western culture and entertainment.

Until now.

Ladies and gentlemen, meet Le Petomane's rightful descendant, Mr. Methane, England's Prince of Poots, who has dedicated his life to following in the footsteps of the great man—though not too closely.

One day in 1982, a fifteen-year-old boy in Macclesfield, Cheshire, named Paul Oldfield, was practicing yoga when he accidentally discovered that if he rolled onto his back from the lotus position, he could suck air into his anus and, better yet, blow it back out again. Le Petomane had likewise stumbled onto his gift a century earlier, while wading in the ocean and suddenly feeling his lower colon filling up with cold water. Looking back now, Oldfield says, it didn't cross his mind at the time that farting could bring him fame and fortune, or at least a little bit of each, so he confined his talents to amusing his buddies. "Apart from a few performances in the school squash court, I did not make use of it," he says in his normal, punctilious way. He followed a more practical path and became a locomotive engineer for British Railways. Still, whenever he showed off at a party or a backyard barbecue, he always got a big laugh. One day a fellow railroad worker shot some video footage and showed it around. Next thing you know, a local rock and roll band called the Macc Lads invited him to open for them at a joint called the Screaming Beavers Club. Just as the great Le Petomane had performed in an elegant outfit—tails, dark pants (with a trap door in back), and stockings—as a counterpoint to the vulgarity of his act, Oldfield spruced up his thin, six-foot-seven frame in a pinstripe suit for his stage debut. His rectal renditions of "Twinkle Twinkle Little Star" and the theme song from a British sports show brought down the house. He rushed out and made up some business cards. He began showing up at parties all around Macclesfield, farting "Happy Birthday."

He developed his Mr. Methane character—a caped hero in a green mask and a matching outfit with an M on the chest—when the Macc Lads took him out on the road. "The Mr. Methane idea came about as a result of needing a name and persona to go on tour," Oldfield says. "Until then I had been billed as 'The Incredible Farting Man from Buxton Shunting Yards' and traded as 'The Bum Notes Fart-a-Gram.' Somehow from all the brainstorming, the idea for Mr. Methane emerged and I had a costume made." He claims he wasn't influenced by Rodger Bumpass's Fartman character from the 1980 *National Lampoon* record album, or by Howard Stern's subsequent purchase of the rights to the character in 1986. "I had never heard of Fartman then." (For a detailed history of Fartman, see the Howard Stern chapter in *Who Cut the Cheese?*)

By 1993, Paul Oldfield had quit the railway and his alter ego, Mr. Methane, had begun touring the pubs of England, billing himself as "The World's Only Performing Flatulist." He even trumpeted "God Save the Queen" on Swedish television. Figuring that maybe his act could use a little extra class, he borrowed some symphonic CDs from the library and practiced farting along with the classics. And yet he felt underappreciated. "I can perform in three tones," he told a newspaper at the time, "but so long as a club audience can have a good laugh and see my bottom, they don't notice which tone I am playing. I need an audience that will let me grow." It's a common complaint among artists great and small—their public doesn't recognize that there's a genius behind the artifice, or in this case the fartifice.

Despite his popularity, Mr. Methane couldn't get an insurance company to cover his ass. "If they could insure Liberace's hands, Betty Grable's legs, and Samantha Fox's breasts, why not my derriere?" Mr. Methane asked. The answer, of course, was that underwriters wouldn't have been able to prove or disprove whether his occupation had been affected by a disability, so there was too great an opportunity for fraud. "It would be as hard to assess a loss of this man's talent as it would a loss of taste for a wine taster," said a representative of the Association of British Insurers.

When Oldfield released his first CD, *mr methane.com*, he included a mixture of self-penned and traditional melodies, punctuated by soliloquies from Shakespeare—though one line he forgot to throw in was Mistress Quickly's quip to Falstaff from *The Merry Wives of Windsor*: "She's as fartuous a civil modest wife, and one, I tell you, that will not miss you morning nor evening prayer, as any is in Windsor." The Shakespeare Birthplace Trust, a charity enacted by Parliament in 1891 to preserve the bard's home and promote his works, wasn't impressed. "I have yet to be persuaded that Mr. Methane's novel approach to reciting well-known passages from Shakespeare will illuminate their meaning or beauty," wrote the society's director, Roger Pringle. He suggested that if Mr. Methane insisted on essaying one of Shakespeare's characters, it should be Nick Bottom, the weaver from *A Midsummer Night's Dream*. (He might also have recommended Francis Flute from the same play.)

In 1999 our hero released a video of his stage performance under the title *Mr. Methane Lets Rip!* With the camera at ringside, Mr. Methane farted along, in tempo and relatively in tune, with classical music (including "The Blue Danube Waltz," but omitting "The Buttcracker Suite"), imitated a pesky bumblebee, created a talcum powder mushroom, breezily snuffed out candles, puffed on a cigarette (adding new meaning to the phrase "Can I bum a smoke?"), and imitated several characters from Robin Hood, all with his talented toot tunnel. For a finale, he stuck a peashooter up his butt and fired a dart at a medicine-ball-sized balloon halfway across the stage. All this horseplay was broken up by a music video for his theme song, "We Love You, Mr. Methane," and footage of him in normal street clothes shocking unsuspecting tourists at the English seaside resort of Blackpool with rip-roaring flatulence (captured surreptitiously in "Sphincter Scope"). Naturally, bad taste and worse puns prevailed throughout. Visit http://fartvideo.com or http://mrmethane.com for a better look.

Mr. Methane made his American debut on Howard Stern's national radio show on February 1, 2000—literally the dawn of a new century of entertainment. Stern had already been spotlighting amateur farters in tournaments to see how many they could blast in a row or within a certain period of time. (Check out chapter 45 for a more detailed history of Stern's crepitation contests.) But Mr. Methane took the art of farting to a new level by tooting the melodies of "Greensleeves" and "Flight of the Bumblebee," along with Deep Purple's 1973 rock classic "Smoke on the Water." But contrary to at least one report, he did not perform the Cranberries' "[Do You Have to Let It] Linger."

When Stern invited him back for an encore a few months later, Mr. Methane revealed the downside of being a celebrity farter. He had wanted to perform Phil Collins's "In the Air Tonight"—retitled "Curry in the Air Tonight"—on Stern's show, but Collins's manager, Tony Smith, had stifled his London air by refusing to give him performance clearance. Smith reportedly told Mr. Methane, "It's a serious song." The rejection was a great disappointment for the caped crepitator, but stoically he kept it locked up inside. (Author's note: since Collins has been making elevator music for years, Mr. Methane is the perfect elevator-clearing artist for his material.)

On February 16, 2001, during a phone interview, Stern told Mr. Methane that he would be talking to his agent about bringing him back to America and producing his one-man show on Broadway. Stern believed that people from around the world would clamor to watch this rectal raconteur fart his repertoire of songs and imitations, and he wanted to be part of the phenomenon. But Stern would have to personally sponsor Mr. Methane with the U.S. Immigration Service and attest that the lively-sphinctered limey was a unique talent who wasn't coming to America to steal someone else's act. During the call, Mr. Methane took the opportunity to perform a quick, illicit version of "In the Air Tonight." (If you feel that listening to an MP3 recording of that performance is a violation of British copyright law, do *not* go to http://farts.com/intheair.htm.)

At the end of 2001, Mr. Methane flew into New York for another highly rated appearance on Stern's radio show. "I am so behind this guy, so to speak," Stern quipped. Mr. Methane plugged his new Christmas CD of "unplugged" music, *Merry Methane: A Feast of Festive Flatulence,* on which he sang and farted along with eleven holiday songs, backed by former members of the rock groups Jethro Tull and Steeleye Span. He also participated in a new quiz show segment called "Name That Fume," as Stern and his sidekicks Robin Quivers, Fred Norris, and Artie Lange tried to guess the songs he was farting. He got his cheeks around some yuletide treasures like "Jingle Bells" and "Silent (But Deadly) Night," which brought tears to everyone's eyes. As Mr. Methane headed out to entertain people on the street, Stern declared, "I am gonna bring him to Broadway. . . . This guy deserves to be seen. He's the greatest superstar that ever lived!" Mr. Methane's segment aired nationally on cable TV's E! channel on January 9, 2002.

Returning triumphantly to Europe, Mr. Methane opened an art exhibit in Switzerland entitled *Smells of the Alps,* in which he performed traditional Swiss songs, first karaoke-style and then with the horn section from the Bern Philharmonic. (No, his ass didn't yodel.) He also appeared on a BBC TV special, blew out the candles on a birthday cake in front of 6,000 people at a gala in Paris, burst a balloon on a woman's head with an ass dart on French TV, toured Australia several times (where he has become a sensation), and finished a TV pilot for a Mr. Methane animation series. More recently, he has been conferring with one of his fans, Irish singer Sinead O'Connor, about doing a parody duet on "Nothing Compares to Poo," a takeoff on her hit song "Nothing Compares 2 U" (with hopes that the song's composer—the artist formerly known as the Artist Formerly Known as Prince—isn't too tight-assed about it).

Since his Macc Lads days, Mr. Methane has also opened for dozens of musical artists, including Kiss of the Gypsy, reggae legend

Desmond Dekker, and the Super Furry Animals. But he says the people who appreciate his act the most are the sound engineers. "Once here in the U.K., a sound tech was killing himself laughing at a show, not because of the farting but because he had a gig working with [singer] Kylie Minogue coming up," he said, "and he was going to give her the same microphone. I think that this sort of sound tech japery, giving the mic to someone of note at a later date, happens quite a bit."

Despite his other successes, Mr. Methane's Broadway show has not come to pass. "I haven't been to the U.S.A. for some time now; the mood has changed considerably post–September 11," he said in late 2005. "But probably more significant is the Janet Jackson incident. Even Howard seems to have been reined in. Once again farting seems to be taboo on the airwaves, which in a sense is a good thing, as that's what gives it the impact and longevity and creates the folklore in many ways."

So please don't worry about Mr. Methane. He's never at loose ends for long.

Chapter 4

CREPITUS EX MACHINA

Back in 1930, Soren Sorensen "Sam" Adams, the New Jersey prankster who invented and marketed Cachoo Sneeze Powder, the Joy Buzzer, and the Dribble Glass, made a really dumb decision: he turned down the rights to a Toronto rubber company's air-filled bladder that, when sat upon, made the sound of a long, loud fart. "The whole idea seemed too indelicate," Adams said in the 1940s, "so I passed it up." Sixty years later, however, when a Florida inventor approached Adams's descendants with a battery-powered farting machine, they were savvy enough not to make the same mistake.

This particular practical joke goes back centuries to the "fool's bladder," a balloon made from a pig bladder that jesters reportedly used to entertain royalty. But it didn't have any commercial value until 1926, when a "musical seat" appeared in a mail-order catalog from Johnson Smith & Company in Wisconsin. Looking like a small drum with a bellows attached, the unwieldy contraption "sounds like you sat on a cat," according to the catalog. A couple of years later, the JEM Rubber Co., in Toronto, came up with a smaller, more joker-friendly, green rubber version with a wooden mouth, which it first called the Poo-Poo Cushion and the Boop-Boop a Doop (inspired by the popular Betty Boop cartoon character and the singer Helen Kane, on whom she was loosely based). Then, around 1932, in the depths of the Depression, when people needed something to whoop about,

JEM renamed its impudent little wheezer the Whoopee Cushion, taken from a then-popular expression for sex or money canonized by Eddie Cantor's 1928 hit record, "Makin' Whoopee." Suddenly, the little fart bag captured the public's fancy. It was this very cushion that Sam Adams had unwisely rejected a couple of years earlier.

As you might expect, the original JEM Whoopee Cushion is fairly rare and valuable today. Collector Stan Timm, who owns one, said recently that the imprint on his 1932 cushion is "quite striking, being a Scottish kilt-clad boy wearing boots with spurs and carrying a rifle. He is also carrying a mischievous smile." This same picture appeared that year in the Johnson Smith novelty catalog. Says Timm, "This was the first time they advertised the Whoopee Cushion and they offered it in two versions—the economy model for 25 cents and the deluxe model for $1.25. We believe the one we have is the deluxe version because instead of just rubber it is made of a rubber-impregnated fabric. If you're wondering, it no longer works. The mouth is brittle and the rest is stuck together."

Now let's fast-forward half a century to a night in 1990 when the idea of bringing barnyard fart technology into the space age sprung into the dreaming brain of a Del Ray Beach, Florida, man named Fred Jarow. "I woke up in the middle of the night," he said later. "I was laughing, but I didn't know why. I'm not sure that I wasn't farting at the same time."

What the world needed, his subconscious had whispered into his inner ear, was a fart machine to replace the Whoopee Cushion. Now that computer chips could reproduce any sound you wanted, why wait for an unsuspecting victim to sit down on a bag of air? Why not set an electronic, remote-controlled booby trap? Jarow himself was in the textile manufacturing business and knew next to nothing about electronics, so he turned to a friend, John Blackman, for help in developing his vision. They came up with a sleek, black, plastic device with a chip that could generate four different fart sounds triggered from twenty feet away, by someone in the next room or outside a window. Some poor slob is sitting there surrounded by his family or a group of stuffy folks he has to impress, and suddenly all these farts are rip-roaring from beneath his part of the table. Oh what fun! Though Jarow and Blackman initially called their invention the

Electronic Whoopee Cushion, they settled on the more direct and precise Fart Machine.

Jarow claims that the toughest part was coming up with just the right sounds. He says that he and Blackman holed up in a recording studio after ingesting plenty of cabbage and beans, but their farts didn't have the proper gusto or audio frequency. They eventually turned to the synthesizer to create some electronic imitations. "Originally, we wanted to have a really long fart, but it sounded too much like a motorcycle," Jarow told the *Village Voice*. "Shorter ones are much more realistic."

Like the Whoopee Cushion, the Fart Machine fit prankster sage Sam Adams's idea of what makes a perfect prank item. In the June 1, 1946, edition of *The Saturday Evening Post*, Adams, then sixty-seven years old, said, "The whole basic principle of a good joke novelty is that it has to be easy and simple to work. If you have to go through a lot of complications to set the stage for the gag, the public will not go for your item. The best idea is to work with an ordinary everyday object that is around the house.

"When I am fooling around with a new idea, I try to picture Mr. Average Man sitting around a cocktail lounge or in somebody's house before their weekly game of poker, and I try to ask myself if this new item will go in that sort of group; so if Person A pulls the gag on Person B, Person B will get a kick out of waiting for Person C to walk in and get the surprise of his life."

In 1999, according to the *Village Voice*, the S.S. Adams Company announced that sales of their electronic Fart Machine had gone over 100,000 units. Business was booming.

One guy used it to perpetrate a fraud. In mid-October of 1998, he phoned Howard Stern's morning radio program, calling himself the Phantom of the Colon, and claimed that he could beat the show's then-current farting champion. But when Stern invited him to the studio to do his act, it quickly became obvious that he wasn't really farting. He had hidden a Fart Machine in his pants.

In recent years, the Fart Machine has become popular in Hollywood. During the filming of *The Score* (2001), actor Edward Norton reported that his costar, Marlon Brando, delighted in figuring out where Robert De Niro was going to be sitting in his various scenes, and would then tape a Fart Machine under the chair. Brando, incidentally, had already delivered one of the classic early farts of American cinema in the 1976 film *The Missouri Breaks,* when his character told Jack Nicholson, "I feel an attack of gas and that could be perilous to both of us!"—followed by a Method fart.

Actor Johnny Depp is also a big fan of the Fart Machine. He used it on the set of *Chocolat* (2000) to break the tension before his smooching scenes with Juliette Binoche, and then again to relax his costars, including several children, during a dinner scene in *Finding Neverland* (2004). In fact, in one of that film's DVD special features called "The Magic of *Finding Neverland,*" as we hear the sounds of farting during dinner, Depp says in a voice-over, "We sort of saved the Fart Machine for certain moments. [Director] Marc [Forster] and I planned it out early on that we needed it to loosen that dinner scene up, so we hid the Fart Machine under the table and waited for the boys' closeups and just started nailing 'em, and it worked like a charm."

During an appearance on ABC's *Jimmy Kimmel Live,* on January 28, 2003, wrestler/actor Dwayne Johnson, better known as the Rock, joked about how he interrupted his love scene with costar Kelly Hu on the set of *The Scorpion King* by activating a few electronic farts.

On the March 14, 2004, edition of ABC-TV's *Primetime,* when host Diane Sawyer asked actress Jennifer Aniston, "Are you an easy laugh?" Aniston replied, "I'm such an easy laugh. I'm the one who has the Fart Machine and the fart sludge and that stuff, and make a pretty big fool of myself laughing ridiculously hard."

Aniston's costar in 2005's *We Don't Live Here Anymore,* Australian actress Naomi Watts, is also quite a fan of the little noisemaker, according to http://teletextnewsletter.co.uk. In a love scene with Mark Ruffalo, "We were up against the tree, completely naked, trying to act this scene in front of all the crew and cameras," said Ruffalo. "And then Naomi, to ease the tension, had a Fart Machine going. You're about to do a scene, and all of a sudden it's like, 'Prrpt, prrt-prrrpt, prrt-prrrpt.' Instant defuse."

Among other practical jokers who have zinged folks with Fart Machines are Cameron Diaz, Leslie Nielsen, and, according to an article in the *New York Daily News,* even President George W. Bush.

"The Fart Machine has been an unprecedented success in the novelty business," says Blackman. "It has been the number-one best-selling gag since 1992 at Spencer Gifts and other gag and novelty outlets. It is sold in fifty countries around the world, and we recently shipped a two thousand-piece order to a palace in Saudi Arabia."

Blackman is now bragging about an even more advanced version, the Fart Machine No. 2. "Pun intended," he says. "[It] has fifteen farts now, and they're louder than ever because we put in our own patented boom-box blaster for better bass response, and you can activate them from one hundred feet away." There's even a Fart Machine with a motion detector; like a land mine, it only needs to be activated and hidden away—until a victim comes by and sets it off. To paraphrase Ralph Waldo Emerson, if you invent a better fart machine, the world will beat a path to your door.

Does that mean the old-fashioned, low-tech gimmicks and gim-cracks are going the way of the rotary dial phone? Hardly. There's still something fiendishly fun about making hands-on fart noises that appeals to the ten-year-old kid in most of us. Whoopee cushions continue to sell in all shapes and colors (even bright colors that would seem to subvert any stealthy prank). There's even a self-inflating cushion, not to mention a Halloween whoopee cushion costume for the discerning trick-or-treater. And then there's the little Fart Bag, which you simply squeeze with your fingers. "With just a bit of practice, you'll be making sweet music with this hand-held Whoopee Cushion," says the Johnson Smith Company catalog ad copy. Actor Leslie Nielsen has even demonstrated the Fart Bag's impromptu qualities on TV for Jay Leno, David Letterman, and Rosie O'Donnell. But clearly, in a nation that loves to fight its wars from a thousand miles away, the idea of blasting farts under people's chairs from the next room or the house next door has an undeniable appeal.

In 2003, veteran television writer-director Daniel Chasin made a mockumentary about Fred Jarow's invention of the Fart Machine, called *It's Tough Being Me*, for Laughing Hyenas Films.

When asked to reveal his own favorite Fart Machine prank, Jarow recalled hiding one in a Thanksgiving turkey. "I hit the remote just as the host began carving."

Now try doing *that* with an old Whoopee Cushion!

Chapter 5

FAUX FARTS IN A FLASK

In January 2003, museum officials at the Dewa Roman Experience in Chester, England, created a stink when they added the appropriate redolence to their reconstruction of a Roman latrine. It was so realistic that several visiting schoolchildren became sick on the spot. "The smell was disgusting. It was like very strong boiled cabbage, sweet and sickly," supervisor Christine Turner said in a BBC interview.

The offending substance, called Flatulence, was a product of Dale Air (www.daleair.com), a company in Kirkham, England, that manufactures "themed aromas"—liquids atomized into the air by hidden dispensers. More specifically, Flatulence was concocted by Dale Air's owner, Frank Knight, who works with a team of perfumers in a one-room lab filled with beakers of sundry smells and a bottling machine. Though he's not a chemist by training, Mr. Knight has formulated the reek of a dead body for an English zoo, the smell of an Egyptian mummy for the City Museum of Stockholm, Sweden, and the odors of a swamp and a Tyrannosaurus Rex's breath for an exhibit in London's Natural History Museum. In all, he has made nearly three hundred different fragrances and stenches, including Granny's Kitchen (which nursing home doctors sometimes use for stimulating the memories of Alzheimer's patients), Havana Cigar, Sweaty Feet, Japanese Prisoner of War, and Old Drifter. But none of them sent people into woozy fits like the vapors of Flatulence.

Though two of his other patented smells, Boiled Cabbage and Rotten Eggs, are part of the recipe, Knight is tight-lipped (and closed-nosed) about the panoply of Flatulence's ingredients. And no wonder—he claims that it's his biggest seller. Recently he added the odor to London's Imperial War Museum's exhibit on World War I trench warfare, where mere Mustard Gas apparently wasn't offensive enough.

"I won't go near [Flatulence] without wearing a white coat and latex gloves," Knight said recently. He made no mention of a gas mask.

Chapter 6

AWARD-WINNING
WIND-CUTTING FOR KIDS

In 2003, the Nickelodeon cable TV channel's Kids' Choice Awards show added a new category, "Favorite Fart in a Movie," even though films had to have at least a relatively kid-friendly PG rating in order to qualify for entry. From early March to April 3 of that year, seventeen million kids voted at Nick.com's ballot page.

Finally the big night—April 15—arrived for the sixteenth annual Kids' Choice Awards, airing live from the Pauley Pavilion at UCLA in Los Angeles.

"And the nominees are . . ." said presenter Ashton Kutcher: "*Austin Powers 3, Master of Disguise, Crocodile Hunter, Scooby Doo.*"

"And the winner is . . ." (dramatic opening of envelope; breaths bated all over America; asses clenched in the audience for fear of upstaging the winner) "*Scooby Doo!*"

Suddenly the award show's producer inexplicably cut to a reaction shot of TV twins Mary-Kate and Ashley Olsen sitting in the audience, which fed all sorts of speculation and created a stink in its own right, but we're not concerned with that here. If the Olsen twins want coverage in this book, they'll have to come up with their own farts—in stereo.

Anyway, *Scooby Doo* was Warner Bros.'s $51-million remake of a popular 1970s TV series from Hanna-Barbera, an animation company known for its barely moving cartoon characters. For the new Hollywood version, real actors stepped into all the roles except for the eponymous Scooby Doo, a talking Great Dane re-created by computer graphics (CG) technology. In the award-winning scene, the dog got into a farting bout with Shaggy, his goofy human companion played by Matthew Lillard. (Lillard had already given the Hollywood press the *Scooby Doo* poop scoop before the movie's June 2002 release when he announced, "Scooby and I actually get into a farting contest. Your kids are gonna love this.") Since Scooby was unavailable for the Nickelodeon event, Lillard ran up onstage alone to accept the award, an orange blimp called the Blimpy—an unwieldy representation of a flying gas bag presented to all Kids' Choice winners, but certainly most appropriate for Favorite Fart.

Pop culture observers who watched the event weren't sure what a farting prize portended for the film industry. "It's a sad movie indeed that tries to offer many funny sequences but only delivers one, and when that sequence is an immature farting competition between a man and a dog, that's when you realize just how unfunny the rest of [*Scooby Doo*] actually is," said online critic Mark Dujsik.

But Hollywood didn't care. The Kids' Choice Awards happens to be one of the loosest and hippest of the countless awards shows that clog TV schedules early each year. Along with the presentation of the fart blimp, there's a celebrity burping contest whose past winners include Cameron Diaz, Justin Timberlake, and Hugh Jackman. And these A-listers are all happy to do it. According to Nickelodeon president Cyma Zarghami, the willingness of celebrities to join the juvenile hijinks is "a testament to how powerful the kids' audience is. This segment [of moviegoers] is really important to the box office." Also, as any ad exec will tell you, it's wise even for actors to establish brand identification early and build a lifelong relationship with consumers.

The following year, on April 3, 2004, the winner of the Blimpy for Favorite Fart in a Movie was *Kangaroo Jack,* again a Warner Bros. movie with a CG character in the lead. This time the award-winning scene, which lasted about a minute, involved two crepitating camels and one of the film's flesh-and-blood stars, Anthony Anderson, who retorted with a camel-worthy fart of his own. The drafty dromedaries must have been off making another movie during the awards, because only Anderson showed up to accept the accolades of a grateful public.

Again, it was a case of kids overruling the critics, who were generally not kind to *Kangaroo Jack*. "Apparently, [the camels'] frequent farting struck someone on the screenwriting team . . . as absolutely hilarious, and so the joke is allotted several minutes (which feel longer)," said PopMatters (http://popmatters.com) reviewer Cynthia Fuchs. "By the time the punch line comes, the joke is past expiration. . . . And matching [Anderson's] bodily functions with those of the ostensibly horrific camels only underlines the film's view of [his character, Louis] as the physical joke butt."

Warner Bros. loved the bad press, however, and took a cue from Nickelodeon; when it released *Kangaroo Jack* on DVD, one of the extras was a featurette called "Behind the Gas," with sound engineer Stevie "Bud" Johnson explaining how he and his assistant came up with "the pure sound we were looking for." According to Johnson, they experimented with a Whoopee Cushion, a Fart Machine, a large Mexican take-out meal, the old hand-in-the-armpit trick, and even the reliable razz using their lips and tongues, but they never revealed exactly what combination they used to create camel farts.

The studio also made sure that when Matthew Lillard returned in *Scooby Doo 2*, he delivered a spectacular, well-choreographed fart dance. Speaking about it to Eric S. Elkins at UnderGroundOnline (http://ugo.com/ugo) in June 2004, Lillard said, "I remember the night before [the scene], in my underwear, I posed in front of the full-length mirror, and . . . you also realize, I've done Shakespeare, and here [I am] doing this fart dance." *Hark! What wind through yonder buttocks breaks?*

Unfortunately, at the eighteenth annual Kids' Choice Awards in 2005, Lillard had to sit on those buttocks all through the show because there was no longer any Favorite Fart Blimpy. Though apparently no parents or religious groups complained publicly about all the body noises, Nickelodeon decided to play it safe and not tempt fate in these dark, perilous times.

Or perhaps the network simply didn't want to reduce the American fart award to its Swedish counterpart. In November

2004, at a separate version of the Kids' Choice Awards airing from Stockholm, a plurality of 100,000 young voters inexplicably chose an exploding underwater mine in *Finding Nemo* as Favorite Fart in a Movie.

Or maybe, as comic Al Franken predicted a decade ago, the government has simply installed a universal "F-chip" to block out all farting on television.

Chapter 7

THE FARTING FEMMES OF
NON-VIRTUOUS REALITY

The trendiest fetish in porno right now is girls farting on your computer. A recent Googling of the term "girls who fart" brought up 1,790 sites on the Internet. "Women who fart" revealed another 1,350, including one specialty-item page called "women who fart into cakes." (Don't ask.) "Farting women" added yet another 1,800. One website features Lizz, a self-proclaimed Queen of Farts (http:// queenoffarts.com) who invites visitors to hear and watch her letting barbecued-bean farts, thundering toilet bowl farts, burbling bathtub farts, even poofed-up-pajamas farts—all caught on live cams and videos. Lizz also features a page of letters from her mostly male club members rhapsodizing about female cheezers they've smelled, heard, or dreamt about.

"I think the most exciting thing men like to see is the sheer embarrassment a woman feels when she accidentally lets one go," says Liz P., Queen Lizz herself, who lives in the San Francisco area. "Or they get excited by seeing just the opposite—a confident woman like me purposely ripping one out for everyone to enjoy. But then you have the fetish guy who associates a woman's farts with face sitting. These men . . . take genuine pleasure in being dominated, treated like a seat cushion, and being smothered by their queen. And hopefully humiliated and forced to receive her royal perfume."

But normally, Ms. P.'s butt-gas business is a little more prosaic. "Believe it or not, the most common requests are for very casual and natural farts, where I am fully clothed," she says. "In all honesty, most of my members don't want to see my naked body at all. It's not the human form that turns them on, but rather the act of farting itself in an everyday situation. If a woman is at work and has to let one go, would she run outside and take all her clothes off and announce her fart? No, she would secretly go to a quiet, secluded corner, slowly let the gas escape, and hope no one hears. Or she would fart accidentally and excuse herself politely. And that is exactly what my 'fart guys' want to see. Like a forbidden act they were not supposed to witness."

She occasionally gets requests that seem odd even to her. "One guy actually asked me to capture a fly, put it in a jar, fart in the jar, then close the lid tightly. Is that crazy, or what? And one guy asked me to fart in a coffee cup, then quickly bring it to my nose so I could smell it. Of course, I always get the good ol' 'fart in the tub' requests, and 'fart on a hard surface.' I guess the farts can be better heard that way."

There's also a legion of Internet mail-order companies offering videos of pretty girls blasting or fizzling into each other's faces, or into the faces of hapless (lucky?) guys. Perhaps the Wal-Mart of wall-to-wall farts is FTC Original Videos, a Japanese company whose movies include *Girls Be Farting*, *My Sweet Farts*, and *Take Farts Oneself*—garbled Japanese English for "let them fart on you." The nubile Nipponese nymphs dress in school uniforms, with white socks and matching white cotton panties that, with luck, stay that way. "Three new girls show her [sic] good farts in this video," according to one ad. "Every Girls [sic] farts are loud and smelly. Pretty faces when fart in video." FTC also has the *Farting Iron Woman* series, starring various airy Amazons. One, Marina Suzuki, boasts, "My farts is greatest!" Another, Ruka Ichinomiya, claims her diet of "bulbs"—garlic—makes her flatulence especially piquant. (See http://bekkoame.ne.jp/ha/dins/onarafetish3english.htm.)

Then there's the American video *Foul Wind: A Face Fart Fiesta* (http://foulwind.com), which features guys and girls equally poking their butts in each other's faces, letting go with windy wallops, and then laughing about it. I must confess that I appear briefly in this video, but only as a voice of temperance and reason, in hopes that when viewers at home try farting into the faces of their significant others, they don't overdo it.

Much of the power of all this feminine butt-fluttering is the reluctance of most women to admit they actually do it. If only they knew that a lusty fart might attract *more* men. Not just lowlife pervs, either. James Joyce based his novel *Ulysses*—considered one of the twentieth century's greatest—on the day in Dublin he met his wife, Nora Barnacle, whose bodily functions transfixed him. "You had an arse full of farts that night, darling, and I fucked them out of you, big fat fellows, long windy ones, quick little merry cracks and a lot of tiny little naughty farties ending in a long gush from your hole," Joyce wrote in a private letter. "It is wonderful to fuck a farting woman when every fuck drives one out of her. I think I would know Nora's fart anywhere. I think I could pick hers out in a roomful of farting women. It is a rather girlish noise not like the wet windy fart which I imagine fat wives have. It is sudden and dry and dirty like what a bold girl would let off in fun in a school dormitory at night. I hope Nora will let off no end of her farts in my face so that I may know their smell also."

In others words, Joyce wanted to take farts oneself.

Though we lack other mammals' hypersensitivity to the smells of sex and territorial marking (otherwise, how could we live together in urban environments?), scientists have assured us for years that pheromones—primal scents hidden within everyone's body odors—still guide our sexual behavior. And now we know that thanks to the "stimulus response," or "conditioned reflex," that Dr. Ivan Pavlov illuminated nearly a hundred years ago, even the *sound* of a virtual fart, without the stink, has potent sexual powers.

Seventeenth-century English poet Samuel Butler perhaps said it best in a poem called "Hudibras" (circa 1664), about a young man named Whachum who composed odes to everything, including his girlfriend's various eructations: "And, when imprison'd air escap'd her / It puft him up with poetic rapture."

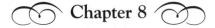

Chapter 8

SPONGEBUTT FARTYPANTS

On Thanksgiving night, 1995, after a huge turkey dinner, Chester "Buck" Weimer was drifting off to sleep when his wife, Arlene, "let go a bomb" that was certainly nothing to be thankful for. Weaker men might have fled the room and filed for divorce the next day, but Buck, a Pueblo, Colorado, resident in his late fifties, was made of sterner stuff. Besides, his wife had been letting off stink bombs for years. She suffered from Crohn's disease, an inflammatory bowel disorder that creates Richter scale–level farts, and Buck—like a man who lived beside the railroad tracks—no longer paid much attention to the nightly rumblings. But on that fateful Thanksgiving night, her gastritis was particularly bad—and under the covers to boot. "I'm laying in bed with her, sort of suffering silently," Weimer remembered with a wince. Something had to be done.

"That's when I came up with my invention for the world's first fart-proof underwear!"

Three years later he patented his own fart-knocker knickers.

The trickiest part was finding a filter that wasn't bulky, but could capture foul-smelling particles while allowing the non-smelling elements of a fart—mostly hydrogen and oxygen—to slip through. The perfect solution turned out to be a coal miner's gas mask filter. After Weimer did a little tweaking in his garage workshop, he was ready to take on the world of unfettered flatulence.

He called his hermetically sealed skivvies Under-Ease. Designed in both men's boxer and women's panty styles, they're made from airtight, polyurethane-coated nylon, with elastic gaskets around the waist and thighs. Gas can only exit from one small, triangular egress in the rump, where Weimer strategically placed his removable filter made of spun-glass material and activated charcoal sandwiched between layers of Australian sheep's wool. (Its exact makeup is a trade secret, because Buck doesn't want any counterfeiters to start making fart-knocker knicker knockoffs, but it's a sure bet that the wool doesn't touch the buttocks.)

Weimer ordered the first run of Under-Ease—750 pairs—from a Denver apparel contractor in early 2001, and within a few months he had to reorder. "Now we're selling approximately eight thousand pair per year," Buck said in early 2006. "The ratio between the briefs and the boxers is approximately 60/40, with the briefs getting the majority." They sell for $24.95; two replacement filters cost $9.95. Under-Ease are washable and last about a year, depending on the frequency of use and laundering. Filters last from several weeks to several months, depending on the noxiousness of the wearer's farts.

From the beginning, the Weimers have had to rely on the anonymity of the Internet (http://under-tec.com). According to Buck, "When we started out with a booth at a health fair here in Pueblo, our brochures flew off the table, but nobody was brave enough to purchase anything in person. Nobody wants to admit to having that problem because of the shame. That's why we do most of our business online."

One elderly lady wrote to say that her recently purchased pairs of Under-Ease had literally been her salvation. She hadn't been to church for two years previously because of her chronic, ungodly flatulence, which had made folks who shared her pew say "P-ew!" They thought she had sold her ass to the Devil.

"We're really trying to help people," says Arlene Weimer, a psychologist when she's not an Under-Ease saleslady. But mostly the product has helped her personally. Her most embarrassing pre-Under-Ease moment, she says, was when a client complained that her office smelled like a sewer and asked if she had plumbing problems. Since trust in a psychologist-client relationship goes both ways, Arlene owned up to her *sang-froidian* slip. (How's that for a visual pun? It only works on paper.)

In October 2001, the Weimers were called to Boston to receive Harvard University's Ig Nobel Prize, which honors imaginative and goofy achievements in science, medicine, and technology. Buck and Arlene also stopped in New York City to appear on the *Howard Stern* show, home of Fartman. "We were kind of skeptical at first," says Buck, "but Howard was sincerely interested in what we were doing. He was funny, but he was respectful, too." In other words, Stern wasn't being a smarty pants.

Chapter 9

SUPERMAN = SUPERFART!

In Swedish, *fart* is the word for "action," which makes Superman on the cover of Swedish comic books look like not just the Man of Steel, but also the Man of Steel Bowels. (I've got my own copy of a Swedish Superman mag with *Super-Fart!* and *Super-Tuff!* emblazoned above the superhero's head.

According to Swedish speaker Noel Benson, *fart* can also be "speed," or "start"—as in *ta fart*, meaning "to get a start"—or force, energy, or activity. "Every parking garage in Sweden is full of *utfarts* and *infarts*," says Benson. "A traffic obstruction or barrier is called a *farthinder* and a speed trap is called a *fartkontroll*." In German, *fahrt* means and sounds roughly the same as the Swedish *fart*, but visually it's not as funny with the *h* in there.

The Swedes' word for an actual fart is *fis*, which is also their name for the musical note F-sharp. It's especially effective when played on a tuba.

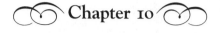

IT WAS A DARK AND STINKY NIGHT

Writers who create nightmares are often impelled by horrific incidents from their childhoods. Charles Dickens's early deprivations drove him to write self-expiating novels about orphans surviving in the poverty-grimed bowels of industrial England. Edgar Allan Poe, wounded by the early death of his consumptive mother, found comfort and catharsis in pining evermore over wraithlike women lying in, or escaping from, their tombs. And Stephen King, the modern king of horror, well, he has a boyhood tale that's almost too scary to contemplate.

His babysitter, a big fat woman, sat on his face and farted!

We're lucky he didn't grow up to be a pervert who went around in a hockey mask on Halloween, farting on the heads of little children.

In his only nonfiction publication, *On Writing: A Memoir of the Craft* (2000)—a cross between an autobiography and a how-to book—Stephen King dredged up this childhood memory: "Eula-Beulah was prone to farts—the kind that are both loud and smelly. Sometimes when she was so afflicted, she would throw me on the couch, drop her wool-skirted butt on my face, and let loose. 'Pow!' she'd cry in high glee. It was like being buried in marsh gas fireworks. I remember the dark, the sense that I was suffocating, and I remember laughing. Because, while what was happening was sort of horrible, it was also sort of funny. In many ways, Eula-Beulah prepared me for literary criticism. After having a two-hundred-pound babysitter fart on your face and yell 'Pow!'—*The Village Voice* holds few terrors."

Don't be fooled by the fact that he's making light of it. Boys, or men revisiting the traumas of their boyhoods, like to light their farts—if only to illuminate the spectral darkness around them.

Beyond inoculating him against literary critics, the experience with Eula or Beulah (he's even suppressed her rightful name, unless her parents actually named her Eula-Beulah) prepared him to write about more than just flammable prom queens, furious Plymouth Furys, and haunted hotels. His fevered imagination also came up with Tommyknockers (which sound suspiciously like fartknockers) and, most tellingly, byrums, or "shit weasels"—the alien creatures in his 2001 novel *Dreamcatcher* that crawl into the lower intestine, create rumbling attacks of explosive gas, and then chew their way out through the asshole in a spray of blood. Tell me the shit weasel isn't a deeply repressed, haunted fart trying to escape from King's pysche, if not from his puckered pooter.

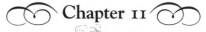

Chapter 11

THE EARTH FARTS BACK

Could a colossal blast of flatulence from gazillions of tiny, unseen critters suffocate civilization as we know it? According to *Discover* magazine, it's possible. "Scientists have discovered that nearly a third of all life on this planet consists of microbes living under the seafloor in a dark world without oxygen," veteran science writer Robert Kunzig observed in 2004. "These tiny creatures make so much methane gas that if even a small proportion of it is released, we might be overwhelmed by tsunamis, runaway global warming and extinctions!"

As researchers probe deeper into the earth, they've found a nether region of primordial, one-celled microbes living as far down as a half-mile beneath the bottoms of the oceans, in what Kunzig calls "astonishing numbers." Relics of an ancient earth where oxygen was rare, they feed upon the muck created by aeons of decaying fauna and flora, and then they expel methane. "These microbes are forming enormous amounts of gas," said Gerald Dickens, a marine geochemist at Rice University. As their micro-farts mix with water and sediment in the deep cold, they form frozen methane hydrate, a semisolid substance that, despite the low temperatures, seethes like a bubbling pot. Scientists claim that this methane hydrate is probably greater than all known reserves of coal, gas, and oil combined. One of the world's most massive deposits, called Hydrate Ridge, lies just off the Oregon coast.

If this gaseous material were disturbed by geological forces and sent toward the ocean's surface, the sea-level pressure would melt the water molecules and release the methane as a huge greenhouse gas bubble or cloud that could possibly create not just havoc, but rapid changes in the climate. "[Methane belches from the depths] may have helped pull the planet out of recent ice ages," claims Kunzig, "and they almost certainly helped end the Paleocene epoch fifty-five million years ago with an intense burst of global warming."

Gregory Ryskin, associate professor of chemical engineering at Northwestern University, believes these methane depth-charges-in-reverse changed the earth much earlier. Writing in the September 2003 issue of the journal *Geology*, Ryskin suggested that huge methane clouds suddenly liberated from deep stagnation could have killed off the majority of marine life and land animals and plants at the end of the Permian era—long before the age of dinosaurs.

By Ryskin's calculation, there are possibly 10,000 gigatons of dissolved methane near the ocean floor under high pressure. If released by an earthquake, a bubble would need only a 5- to 15-percent mixture of oxygen-methane concentration to become explosive, with a force 10,000 times greater than the world's entire stockpile of nuclear weapons. "That amount of energy is absolutely staggering," said Ryskin. "As soon as one accepts this mechanism, it becomes clear that if it happened once it could happen again. I have little doubt there will be another methane-driven eruption—though not on the same scale as 251 million years ago—unless humans intervene." Ryskin believes that dissolved methane, along with dissolved carbon dioxide (which alone killed 1,700 people and livestock near Cameroon's Lake Nyos in a 1986 eruption) and hydrogen sulfide, could create enough dust and vaporized sulfur smog to make the earth uninhabitable.

So beware of all those eensy-teensy-weensy farts massing together under the sea, ready to come and get us!

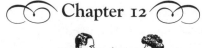

Chapter 12

THE FICKLE FINGER OF FARTS

"Pull my finger!"

According to *The Babe,* the 1992 biopic of baseball legend Babe Ruth, "pull my finger" was Ruth's favorite joke, not to mention a screenwriter's shorthand for emphasizing the home-run slugger's crude, hardscrabble beginnings and his good-natured rapport with his fans. Along with an autograph, he was likely to offer his finger and give his admirer a clubhouse-clearing souvenir.

"Pull my finger" is perhaps the best-known catchphrase in the world of wind-breakers, more common even than "Who cut the cheese?" Someone, usually a friend or family member, extends a forefinger and invites you to give it a yank. But like most jokes, it's good only once per customer. After you've tugged and received a fart for your effort, you probably won't do it the next time.

We know that the middle finger salute, also called "giving the finger" or "flipping the bird," goes back a couple thousand years. The *digitus infamis* or *digitus impudicus* (infamous or indecent finger) showed up occasionally in the literature of ancient Rome. "Laugh loudly, Sextillus, when someone calls you a butt boy, and stick out your middle finger," the first-century poet Martial wrote in *Epigrams II, 27*. In case you don't know, giving someone the finger means either "fuck you" or "up your ass," shortened in American and British parlance to "up yours."

But the origin of the *digitus fartus tuggus* (okay, I made that one up) is hard to get a firm grip on. I'd like to think that God is telling Adam, "Pull my finger," in Michelangelo's *Creation of Adam* on the ceiling of the Vatican's Sistine Chapel—but if the artist included a talk balloon saying as much, Pope Julius II must have made him paint over it. As I pointed out in *Who Cut the Cheese?* we do know that the extended hand or finger has been around since at least the nineteenth century. Émile Zola referred to it in his 1887 novel, *The Earth*, when a windy fellow named Jésus-Christ proffered his hand to his daughter and said, "Pull hard, draggle-tail! Make it go off with a bang!" Was she jerking on only one finger or several, and if only one, which one? Again, we don't know.

Regardless, "pull my finger"—meaning the forefinger—has become the rage in the twenty-first century.

Musically, there's a waltz titled "Pull My Finger," recorded by Wisconsin's Da Happy Schnapps Combo Polka band. In Canada, Pull My Finger, an indie rock band from Vancouver, has an album titled *Let Er Rip*, and comics Bowser & Blue sing "Pull My Finger," the highlight of their 2004 *Pull My Finger* CD.

Canada is also the home of "Pull My Finger," an award-winning TV commercial for an Internet boutique beer seller (http://beer.com) that ran several years ago. It was a spoof of all those earnest Internet company ads from the dot-com boom era, when idealistic young entrepreneurs wanted to show the people of the world working together in cross-cultural cyber harmony. Its punch-line scene was an African villager offering his finger to a loved one. When she gave it a pull, a flock of birds frantically flapped into the air from a tree directly behind him.

On NBC's popular *Friends*, one of the lead characters, Chandler (Matthew Perry), extended his finger a couple of times. For example, in the episode entitled "The One with Joey's Award" (Season 7, Episode 18), Monica (Courtney Cox) says, "Hey sweetie, come here! Come sit down. Hey, Phoebe and I were just talking about how our relationship is deep and meaningful. It really is, don't you think?"

Chandler responds, "Oh, totally! Pull my finger."

The toot tug has also invaded Japan, if director Yasujiro Ozu's *Good Morning,* with its young brothers in suburban Tokyo engaging in a finger-plucking competition, is any indication.

Then there's the 1999 "musical toot" CD called *Pull My Finger,* featuring ninety-nine tracks of assorted fartings with corresponding names like "Heiny Hiccup," "Bugle Boy," "Donald Loves Daisy [Duck]" (you can imagine what that one sounds like), "Dotting the I," "Champagne Cork," "Colon POWel," and "Slide Trombone," plus a musical salute to Christmas called "Silent Butt Deadly Night." According to producer Richard Halpern, *Pull My Finger* (http://pullmyfinger.com) has sold over 250,000 units. Its 2001 sequel, *Pull My Finger 2: Barfs, Farts & Belches,* included even more farts, along with two fart-along tunes: "Crapper's Delight" and John Philip Sousa's "Stars & Stripes Forever." "This time we miked a couple of toilet bowls, including the one at a sandwich shop near our studio," says Halpern. "We didn't have to add any echo; it was all natural." Currently he's hawking *Pull My Finger Vol. 3: Smelly Holiday,* which includes tracks like "The 12 Farts of Xmas" and "Sugarplum Farties."

The first album's rip-roaring success led Halpern to move to Hollywood and co-produce a forty-five-minute documentary film called, oddly enough, *Pull My Finger*—the story of his national Pull My Finger tour in early 2000, during which he visited not just the *Howard Stern* show, but also the *Donny & Marie* [Osmond] show, a syndicated talk program. "It's really the story of my passion to get on the Stern show," says Halpern. "I had a tough time getting on until I came up with the idea of bringing on two fat girls who could fart on cue. Gary [Dell'Abate, the producer] loved it, and that's what finally got us [Halpern and his production partner, Dan Rogers] booked, but then we had to find two fat girls and come up with an elaborate way to get them to fart." Their segment, like a pointed finger, almost got pulled while they were still in the green room, when Dell'Abate insisted that the girls prove they could fart before he'd let them go on the air, and only one of the girls was able to squeeze one off. They did make it onto the show, but Stern was unenthusiastic. "The best thing that came out of our appearance," says Halpern, "was that Donny Osmond called me to say he heard the show and loved it. I sent him three hundred CDs to pass around to his friends, and that led to us getting on the *Donny & Marie* show. The most amazing thing is that we got a lot more response from being on *Donny & Marie* than we did from *Howard Stern,* though to be fair we did pretty well after Howard asked us to come back a second time." Halpern originally hoped to license footage from popular movies to show how flatulence has become a big crowd-pleaser over the past quarter-century, but he ultimately settled on just one scene: the farting cowboys from Mel Brooks's 1974 classic *Blazing Saddles.* Furthermore, to give the film *Pull My Finger* a patina of respectability and intellectual weight, Halpern and Rogers interviewed yours truly to get a historical perspective. "The documentary is finished and ready to go, but what's holding it up is getting the licensing rights for Howard's E! show," Halpern says. "Really, all the events lead up to that first appearance, and without it the movie would be incomplete." In the meantime, he's working on other film projects (www.bluedaniel.com/zzyzx/) and a new Pull My Finger game in which "farticipants" have to name famous melodies performed by fart samples.

"Pull my finger" has also become a buzz phrase on the lucrative gadget and prank circuit, thanks to Pull My Finger Fred, a loquacious doll with an extended digit, sitting in his recliner as he dispenses farts along with such verbal gems as "Bombs away!" and "Who stepped on a duck?" (Fred's voice belongs to a Chicago voice-over artist named Mark MacLean.) According to Geoff Bevington, Fred's co-creator (along with Jamie Wirt), "For a company built on the premise of one idea—a farting doll—we've grown considerably." He says their Illinois-based company, Tekky Toys (http://tekkytoys .com), has sold over 300,000 units worldwide and has spawned an ever-growing family of Pull My Finger dolls, including Freddy Jr., George W. Bush, Fat Bastard (from the *Austin Powers* movies), Santa Claus, Count Fartula, and Fartenstein. "We have a lot of pull in this industry," Bevington deadpans.

Wait a second, is he pulling my leg?

⌒⌒ Chapter 13 ⌒⌒

BEST-SELLING DOG FARTS AT MAN!

Dog bites man, that's not news. But when a farting dog makes the *New York Times* Book Review section, that's a sound bite.

On April 15, 2004, a forty-page children's book called *Walter the Farting Dog*—the story of a lovable but gassy family pet who can't even gobble down a bag of low-fart dog biscuits without stinking up the house—went to number one on the *New York Times* list of best-selling books. It also topped the reading charts at the *Boston Globe* and *Publishers Weekly*. "[Walter] can't help it," said the ad line from the publisher, North Atlantic Books. "It's just the way he is. Fortunately, Billy and Betty love him in spite of it. But their father says he's got to go! Poor Walter, he's going to the dog pound tomorrow."

Fortunately for Walter, the authors had seen the film *Home Alone*, so they introduced a couple of hapless burglars who break into the house the night before the hound is bound for the pound and, well, you know what happens next, even if you haven't forked over $15.95 for this skimpy book. Walter chases the poot-phobic perps, "choking and gasping for air," into the clutches of the police.

Funny, I don't remember Dick and Jane having such problems with Spot. There was never "Look, Jane, see Spot fart."

Walter the Farting Dog had first been published two-and-a-half years earlier, in late 2001, for kids from four to eight, but their parents, who apparently remembered their own crepitating canines from childhood (or at least the family pets who took the rap for every fart in the house), embraced it, too. The book became so popular it was translated into several languages, including Latin (*Walter Canis Inflatus*).

Two *Walter the Farting Dog* sequels followed. The first was *Trouble at the Yard Sale* (2004), in which Walter ends up in the hands of a thief who tricks him into blowing up balloons with a special "fart catcher" by telling him they'll be used at a children's party. But what the guy is really planning to do is take the balloons into a bank and burst them to overwhelm the tellers with clouds of choking gas. Then came *Rough Weather Ahead* (2005), the story of what happens when a special doggie diet food that's supposed to cure Walter's flatulence only makes it worse. Walter's digestion gets so bad that he bloats up like a balloon, floats out the window, and hovers in the sky for days, until he's able to release all the hot gas inside him to save millions of butterflies trapped in a freezing windstorm.

"All in all, it's a gas," said *Booklist*, without mentioning that the book's most dramatic scene may have been inspired by Cervantes's prologue to the second part of his sixteenth-century masterpiece, *Don Quixote*, in which a madman goes to the center of Seville, gathers a crowd, grabs the rear legs of a stray dog, inserts one end of a hollow reed into its anus, puts the other end in his mouth, and starts blowing. The crowd watches, transfixed, as the dog inflates like a balloon. When its belly is grossly round and full, the man lets it run away, with air escaping in a noisy rush from its ass. Then he turns to the crowd and asks, "How think you, my masters, is it a small matter to blow up a dog like a bladder?"

Walter the Farting Dog has inspired similar children's books. When the two *Walter* sequels moved to Dutton Books's juvenile division, North Atlantic Books replaced him with *Little Lord Farting Boy*, about a flatulent bear named Arty, written by one Scootchie Turdlow. Then there's *Pee-Ew! Is That You, Bertie?* by David Roberts (published in 2004 by Harry N. Abrams), about a boy whose farting is so plentiful and odoriferous, everybody else feels free to fart in his presence because they can put the blame on him. Meanwhile, the sales of earlier children's books like Francisco Pittau's *Terry Toots*, Taro Gomi's *Everyone Poops*, Susan K. Buxbaum and Rita G. Gelman's *Body Noises*, and Shinta Cho's *The Gas We Pass* have picked up. I guess it's time I dusted off my own manuscripts for a couple of sure-(butt) fire kiddie classics called *My Pet Pet Goes Putt Putt* and *I Tawt I Smelt a Pooty Tat!*

So how does one create a stinky, gassy best seller for preschoolers? In the case of *Walter the Farting Dog,* it helps if one half of the writing team is William Kotzwinkle, whose previous books include the novelizations of *E.T. the Extra-Terrestrial* and *Superman III.* The other half is a Canadian educator named Glenn Murray. Audrey Colman's clever, surreal illustrations also contributed mightily to the book's success. Still, getting *Walter* published was a struggle that took nearly ten years. "We were surprised by the strength of the resistance," Murray told writer Heidi Henneman. Publishers, though amused, thought the subject was too controversial for the children's market. But Murray, the father of two sons, knew his book would be a great educational tool. "Little boys love trucks, dinosaurs, and farts," he said. "It's so important to hook them [on reading] very early."

Now, with a movie deal in the works and an "action figure" on the market, one thing is certain: we haven't smelled the last of Walter.

Chapter 14

IT'S STINKY, IT'S YUCKY,
IT'S ICKY, IT'S YOU!

Now that *Walter the Farting Dog* has set the bar high, teachers, librarians, and museum curators are grossing out little children with butt boom-booms and other bodily functions, much to the delight of parents.

It's all part of a new "kid science" called Grossology, the study of effluvium and effluents created by our bodies. In the words of writer and former science teacher Sylvia Carol Branzei-Velasquez, "Sometimes it's stinky. Sometimes it's crusty. Sometimes it's slimy. But hey, it's your body."

In May of 2004, at the Discovery Science Center in Santa Ana, California, a stage show called *Gross Me Out!*—designed to teach kids about "the grossest thing in the world: our bodies"—drew 1,200 people over the weekend and became the center's most popular draw since it opened six years earlier. The mistress of ceremonies, who called herself Sally Snot, asked everyone about such things as the cause of flatulence. "The kids love it," center spokeswoman Lisa Segrist told the *Los Angeles Times*. "Especially the little ones."

At the same time, Branzei-Velasquez assured critics that Grossology "has nothing to do with being gross. It's a hook to draw [kids] into science and reading." She trademarked the term to market the lesson plans and exhibits (including "Y U Stink") she first put together in 1993, but in the dozen years since, Grossology has grown to include a new genre of children's books, including those in which turds and wads of snot are the main characters. Her own book, *Grossology*, originally released in 1995 and reprinted by a larger company seven years later, has spawned several sequels.

Branzei-Velasquez says kids vote constantly for their favorite gross-out topics on her website (http://grossology.org). Flatulence has been a longtime favorite, but in 2004 diarrhea ("the worst of number two") replaced it at number one. "I want to get [kids] feeling good about science," she says.

I certainly support her efforts. After all, her kids will eventually graduate to *Who Cut the Cheese?* and *Blame It on the Dog*.

Chapter 15

HERE I SIT ALL BROKENHEARTED

It sounded like a bad joke. In fact, it sounded like the West Virginia joke I told in *Who Cut the Cheese?* about nobody in the family telling Granny that they were going to dynamite the old, rotting outhouse in back and replace it with a new one. "Whooo-eee!" Granny shouted right after the blast, straightening her wig as she sat in a puddle of shit twenty feet away from where the outhouse once stood. "I'm glad I didn't let *that* one in the house."

But this time it was real—and in West Virginia, no less, not far from my old Morgantown stomping grounds. On July 13, 2004, John Jenkins, a fifty-three-year-old employee of North West Fuels Development in Blacksville, eased himself down on the seat of a portable toilet. Ah, nothing like a respite from the toils and cares of the day. He put a cigarette between his lips and pulled out his trusty Zippo. "When I struck the lighter," Jenkins later told the Associated Press, "the whole thing just detonated—the whole top blew off. I can't tell you if it blew me out the door or if I jumped out."

The flame had ignited methane gas leaking from a pipeline beneath the toilet that had been damaged by heavy equipment running over it.

Jenkins sued everybody—including the contractor that operated the heavy equipment and the coal company that owned the property—for $10 million. He had spent over a week at the burn unit of Ruby Memorial Hospital in Morgantown, getting skin grafts on his forearms. But perhaps the greatest injury was to his pride when the Associated Press beamed the story around the world: "Man Injured in Toilet Blast Files Suit!"

I'm not privy to all the facts, but the respondents have so far refrained from suggesting to the court that maybe the plaintiff just happened to let one hell of a fart.

What makes Mr. Jenkins's story even more fantastic than it seems is that the exploding toilet has been a running joke for many years now, as well as an urban legend. Normally these shithouse shenanigans feature a wife throwing or spritzing a flammable liquid into the toilet, followed by the unsuspecting husband sitting down, lighting a cigarette, and creating a pyrotechnic finale that's detrimental to the health of his butt cheeks. According to the urban myth debunkers at the San Fernando Valley Folklore Society (http://snopes.com), the liquid can be paint thinner (toxic waste disposal), pesticide (to kill a scary bug), a powerful cleaning solvent (gasoline or worse), hairspray, or cheap perfume, just as long as it's highly combustible. The writers of the NBC television series *L.A. Law* even recycled the joke into an episode called "Smoke Gets in Your Thighs," which aired originally on November 15, 1990. Douglas Brackman (Alan Rachins), head of the show's law firm, went to the men's room right after someone had painted the walls and dumped the used turpentine into the toilet. Brackman sat down and lit a cigarette, and explosive drama ensued.

Dr. Jan Harold Brunvand, a folklorist who's written several books on urban legends, as well as the introduction for a children's book by Catherine Daly-Weir called *The Exploding Toilet: Tales Too Funny to Be True,* says the story was originally a rural gag about outhouses before indoor plumbing came along, and even then the victim was usually a husband or grandfather who sat down on the wooden oval, gazed contentedly out the small half-moon window in the door, and lit his corncob pipe, not realizing that one of the womenfolk had just finished cleaning the walls with some old gasoline and then dumped the remainder down the hole.

The joke was in fact enshrined by poet Robert Service, the Scottish roustabout who chronicled the American West. In "The Three Bares" (1949), he wrote that Ma disposed of some used benzene down the middle hole of the outhouse. The next morning, after a hearty breakfast, Grandpa "sniffed the air and said: 'By Gosh! how full of beans I feel.'" He hurried down the path to the crapper, sat down inside with the full intention of meditating, lit his pipe, and dropped the match down into the fumes. Hearing the explosion, Ma immediately realized what had happened:

> So down the garden geared on high, she ran with all her power,
> Behold the old rapscallion squattin' in the duck pond near,
> His silver whiskers singed away, a gosh-almighty wreck,
> Wi' half a yard o' toilet seat entwined about his neck. . . .
> He cried: "Say, folks, oh, did ye hear the big blow-out I made?
> It scared me stiff—I hope you-uns was not too much afraid?
> But now I best be crawlin' out o' this dog-gasted wet. . . .
> For what I aim to figger out is—WHAT THE HECK I ET?"

What initially arouses skepticism about poor John Jenkins's misfortune is that the media ran a similar story in the past that turned out to be false. In 1988, the wire services Reuters and United Press International picked up a specious item from the *Jerusalem Post* about a bug-phobic Israeli housewife scooping up a big, nasty-looking cockroach, tossing it into the shitter, and, to make sure the critter was dead, spraying it with a full can of insecticide. We all know what happened when her husband came home. Tossing his cigarette down between his legs, he "seriously burned his sensitive parts," according to the newspaper, and oy! the *schmutz* was everywhere! Only later, after the story ran all over the globe, did the truth come out. "The [Jerusalem] *Post* was not the victim of a deliberate hoax," the editor said in a statement. "Rather, a good tale got so tangled in the telling that it assumed a newsworthiness it should never have had."

More recently, in April 1998, several news agencies picked up an item about a German camper who died just outside Montabaur, near Bonn, when an outhouse exploded as he lit a cigarette and propelled him through a closed window. The cause was either gas leaking from the septic tank or a defective natural gas pipe. Was this story true, or a hoax like the report from Israel? Either way, it sounds like John Jenkins's real-life gas attack in West Virginia.

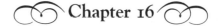

Chapter 16

GOOD OLD HOLLYWOOD
RAZZMATAZZ

"First they moved (1895)!
"Then they talked (1927)!
"Now they smell!"

So said the ad for Michael Todd Jr.'s 1960 whodunit *Scent of Mystery*, which introduced Smell-O-Vision, a process of releasing atomized fragrances into a movie theater to match what was happening up on the screen.

But the blurb could also describe the hundreds of stinkers that Hollywood pumps out every year.

No wonder an aficionado of bad movies named John Wilson decided back in 1980 that it was time to honor Hollywood's most execrable crap in the only way the film industry knows how: with an awards show. He called it the Golden Raspberry Awards, or the Razzies for short.

In *Who Cut the Cheese?* I talked about the *raspberry*, an orally mimicked fart created by sputtering air with the tongue and lower lip. The term comes from London cockney slang, in which words were rhymed and then their sources hidden. For example, the word *dick* (penis) was known as *hampton*—or *'ampton*, as the cockneys would say it. The original rhyme was *hampton wick* (for a borough in London), but by dropping the *wick* (as in "So I pulls out me 'ampton"), they effectively severed *hampton*'s connection to *dick* for any eavesdropping outsider.

In the same way, as early as the 1870s, cockneys turned farts into *raspberry tarts*, and then dropped the *tarts*. When Americans got hold of the cockney *raspberry*, they changed the spelling to *razzberry* and sometimes broke it in half. You could give someone either "the razz" or "the berry"—both were fart imitations—and *razz* was also extended to mean teasing or heckling, since people generally used the razz to show displeasure or contempt. A fart-sounding toy with a wooden mouthpiece attached to a flat rubber tube is called a razzer. It was used on a 1942 million-selling Spike Jones recording called "Der Fuehrer's Face," an anti-Hitler novelty whose chorus was "And we'll [razz! razz!] right in der Fuehrer's face."

As a side note, the original English term for the razz was the *buzz*, or *buzzer*, which showed up in Act II of Shakespeare's *Hamlet*, when the Danish prince invited a donkey-riding theatrical troupe to his castle to reenact the murder of his father.

POLONIUS: The actors are come hither, my lord.
HAMLET: *Buz, buz!*
POLONIUS: Upon my honor,—
HAMLET: Then came each actor on his ass,—

But thanks to the rise of the razz in the twentieth century, the buzz is no longer the bane of every bad actor, but rather what everyone in Hollywood today is desperately seeking.

All of which brings us back to the Razzie Awards®, handed out each year twenty-four hours before the Oscar® broadcast by the Hollywood-based Golden Raspberry Foundation. According to John Wilson, the Razzies® reward the film industry's worst achievements, offer discerning cinephiles an antidote to the fawning and self-congratulatory Academy Awards® ceremonies, and illustrate just how silly and pretentious that goddamn ® is. (The symbol for "registered trademark," it looks like it belongs on the haunch of a Texas steer, not attached to the name of a golden trophy celebrating the Hollywood art of kissing its own ass.) So what better way to scorn Tinseltown movies and the people who make them than by figuratively saying—to quote John Cleese's famous line from the 1975 film *Monty Python and the Holy Grail*—I fart in your general direction!

"When I registered the term with the Library of Congress in 1980," says Wilson, "they asked me, 'Why *raspberry*? What's the significance of that?'" *Razz* was then not as commonly used as *Bronx cheer*—coined many years ago at New York's Yankee Stadium, where baseball fans were prone to making fart noises at the umpires. "But since then, *razz* has pretty much permeated the culture," Wilson boasts, then adds magnanimously, "We couldn't have done it without Hollywood's help."

Incidentally, one film experience that would have rated a loud raspberry if the Razzies had been around twenty years earlier was the aforementioned *Scent of Mystery.* The movie itself was probably not lousy enough to garner an award, but Smell-O-Vision—a system whereby garlic, pipe smoke, and other scents were pumped into the air from tiny plastic tubes hidden under the theater seats—turned out to be one of Hollywood's biggest stink bombs. The machine made an audible hissing sound, and not everyone in the audience got the scents at the same time or at the same intensity. One critic suggested that the only future for Smell-O-Vision lay in dosing the audience with laughing gas. Proving that some things are best left to the imagination, Smell-O-Vision evaporated quickly and was never used again.

To keep the Razzies fresh as they head into the second twenty-five years, Wilson hopes he can come up with new ways to tell the film industry to pull his finger. "Right now I'm thinking about adding the sounds of people farting movie themes on our website" (www.razzies .com), he says.

At last year's Razzie Awards, held on February 26, 2005, at a former burlesque joint called the Ivar Theater, Halle Berry was fingered as Worst Actress for her role in Warner Bros.'s *Catwoman,* which also got razzed for the Worst Film, Worst Director, and Worst Screenplay of 2004. President George W. Bush got the Worst Actor Razzie for his performance in Michael Moore's *Fahrenheit 9/11,* with Defense Secretary Donald Rumsfeld garnering Worst Supporting Actor honors. The only winner with enough aplomb to show up and graciously accept her award was former Oscar winner Halle Berry. You might say that Berry got her Razzie and the Razzie folks got their Berry.

Wilson says there are currently seven hundred voters from around the world, including industry insiders, film critics, and just plain movie fans who like to make rude noises in theaters. The Razzies are often described as "tongue-in-cheek," but in fact one must first remove the tongue from the cheek in order to give a raspberry. In fact, the Razzie has gained enough stature that it's become a kind of media standard for Hollywood awfulness. For example, to underscore the overall ineptitude of actress-screenwriter Jenny McCarthy's *Dirty Love* (2005), critic Richard Roeper said, "They'll need a whole new category in the Razzies." The *Los Angeles Times* began its review of the film with, "Attention, Razzie voters!" (*Dirty Love* did win a buttful of Razzies earlier this year.) The award—a really cheap-looking, golfball-sized raspberry on top of a mangled Super 8 film reel, whose gold veneer looks like it was spray-painted on at a skid row chop shop—has an estimated street value of $4.97. Besides Miss Berry, hardly ever do the winners show up, which goes to show you what a bunch of sore winners Hollywood's A-listers really are. Or maybe they take it personally when the rabble makes farting noises at them.

Chapter 17

HABIT-FORMING FRITTERS

Ah, those French. Where else would a certain kind of dark brown cheese be called *crottin*—or horse turd?

But a more popular item is their *pet de nonne,* or nun's fart— a dainty, sugar-dusted fried fritter. It's also less commonly called a *soupir de nonne* (nun's sigh) and a *pet de soeur* (sister's fart).

The nun's fart is related to the donut, whose origins go back to a Dutch pastry from the fifteenth century called an *olykoek* (oily cake), so named because it was cooked in oil. According to legend, a nun living in the abbey of Marmoutier (wherever that is) was preparing food for a religious feast when she let a fart slip out in the presence of several other nuns. Embarrassed by her faux pas, she dropped a spoonful of dough into a large pot of boiling oil and accidentally made a fritter.

More likely somebody affixed the name simply because of the little pastry's airy texture and sweet scent. Since nuns were thought to eat plain, godly food in meager portions, jokes typically had them farting in hushed wisps under all those garments. Probably more than one viewer of late-1960s television's *The Flying Nun* wondered if what was keeping Sister Bertrille (Sally Field) aloft was too many of those wisps accumulating inside her starched habit.

Since I'd like you to have the pleasure of inviting people over to sample some nun's farts, here's a recipe that will provide you with about forty of them.

Habit-Forming Fritters

PETS DE NONNE (NUN'S FARTS)

6 tablespoons butter

2 teaspoons sugar

1 pinch salt

1 teaspoon grated lemon rind

4 eggs

1 cup flour

1 teaspoon vanilla

1 teaspoon dark rum (optional)

Oil

Confectioners' sugar

In a saucepan, mix the butter, sugar, salt, and lemon rind with 1 cup of water, and bring it slowly to a boil.

While you're waiting, break the eggs into a separate small dish and have them ready.

When the butter has melted, remove the pan from the heat and stir in all the flour at once with a wooden spoon, first carefully, and then after the flour has been absorbed, vigorously.

When you have a thick paste, return the pan to the heat, and turn it up to medium-high. Cook the mixture for 3 to 4 minutes, stirring constantly and scraping the sides and bottom of the saucepan, until the batter clumps together in a solid mass and looks glossy. Take the pan from the stove.

Beat in the vanilla and, if you have it, the rum. When the batter has cooled a little, make a depression in its center, pour in 1 egg, and beat it into the mass. Then beat in the other eggs, one by one, the same way. The batter should now be soft, yet firm enough to hold its shape. Set it aside and let it rest for about 45 minutes.

To maintain the spirit of things, say a few Hail Marys while you're waiting.

Now fill a deep skillet or deep-fat fryer two-thirds full of oil, and heat to 360°F. If you've got a fryer, use a slotted spoon or a wire mesh skimmer, not the basket. Drop the batter into the hot oil one teaspoonful at a time, dipping the spoon into the oil after each scoop. Don't put in too much, because the dough puffs up to about four times its original size, and you'll suddenly find yourself with an opera diva's fart. Nudge the fritters over to color them evenly on all sides.

When they're golden brown, let them drain on paper towels and sprinkle them with confectioners' sugar. Serve hot.

As with any traditional dish, there are many variations of nun's farts. Cajuns more typically call these pastries *pets de soeurs,* use ample amounts of lard, and mix in plenty of cinnamon. Other names include *bourriques de soeurs* (nuns' belly buttons) and *bourriques de viarges* (virgins' belly buttons). The Germans also have fritters called *Nonnenfurzen* (nuns' farts), but they fill theirs with cream or jam.

Speaking of Germans, they make a bread so heavy that it can produce hellacious flatulence that may require an exorcist. The English translation for its name is "devil's fart," which may account for why Americans use the German word instead: *pumpernickel,* taken from *pumpen* (to fart) and *nickel* (a goblin or devil).

WANTED: FART SNIFFERS,
NO EXPERIENCE NECESSARY

It's probably tough enough being an odor judge in the research labs of mouthwash companies, testing their products by getting gargle-scented halitosis breath exhaled directly into your face. But Dr. Michael Levitt, a gastroenterologist at the Veterans Affairs Medical Center in Minneapolis, has taken this drudge job to a whole new level—down to the other end of the long and winding road of human digestion. According to *Popular Science* magazine, in early 2005, Levitt hired two hardy souls to smell other people's farts. "Levitt refuses to divulge the remuneration," staffer William S. Weed wrote, "but it would seem safe to characterize it thusly: not enough."

Under Levitt's guidance, sixteen healthy volunteers ate pinto beans and inserted small plastic tubes into their anuses; after each "episode of flatulence, Levitt syringed the gas into a discrete container, rigorously maintaining fart integrity," according to Weed, a journalist determined to get to the bottom of the story. The two judges then received at least a hundred air samples, opened the caps one at a time, took a nice breath (well, a breath), and rated each fart's noxiousness. Levitt also chemically analyzed each sample and discovered that the worst smelling part of a fart was hydrogen sulfide.

(You have to wonder if the two judges put this job on their resumes. I can see one of them applying for his next position; the interviewer looks up nonplussed and says, "You seem like a real fart smeller, er, I mean, a real smart feller." In English, we call this transposition of first

55

parts of words a *spoonerism,* named for an absentminded reverend, W. A. Spooner, who was prone to saying things like, "It's kisstomary to cuss the bride." But the French call these verbal accidents *contrepeterie,* which literally means "cross-farting.")

Anyway, despite skepticism from many quarters, Dr. Levitt, who's one of the world's top authorities on flatulence (see *Who Cut the Cheese?*), insists that he isn't just farting around. Though gastroenterology is the study of stomach and bowel ailments, he says that up until now his fellow practitioners have never analyzed colon gas to diagnose medical problems. "The odors of feces and intestinal gas and breath could all be important markers of gastrointestinal health," he claims. Hydrogen sulfide, for instance, is very toxic and could lead to ulcerative colitis, among other ailments.

Perhaps the Greek doctor Hippocrates, for whom the Hippocratic oath is named, was right after all when he wrote in 420 BC, "[It] is better for gas to pass with noise than to be intercepted and accumulated internally." In other words, keep farting as if your life depended on it.

As for future jobs requiring professional fart smellers, well, I understand that they're being outsourced to Third World countries.

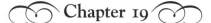

Chapter 19

A BLAST FROM THE PASTURE

It's official. You can stop badmouthing bovine butt gas.

True, methane molecules and light waves vibrate at the same rate, causing methane to absorb more of the sun's energy and create about 20 percent of global warming.

True, methane concentrations have more than doubled in the past one hundred years, and the U.S. Environmental Protection Agency (EPA) estimates that all livestock are responsible for 25 percent of America's methane emissions.

True, the average cow is responsible for producing about 634 quarts of methane a day.

True, there are about 1.3 billion cows munching vegetation all over the world—more than double the 1970 population—and collectively putting nearly 100 million tons of methane into the atmosphere each year.

But now scientists are claiming that despite a lot of lampoon-tinged news items and cow flatulence jokes over the past decade, the main culprit is burping, not farting. I may have even overstated the problem myself in my mini-chapter "Farts May Be the Death of Mankind" in *Who Cut the Cheese?*

According to a June 2003 article in the *Los Angeles Times*, scientists now estimate that 96 percent of cow-generated methane comes from the front end, not the back. Good old Elsie has four stomachs (including a big one that holds forty-two gallons of material) and a chronic case of indigestion. She's constantly chewing, digesting, and regurgitating each meal over and over again—and every time she belches, she expels methane, thanks to an intestinal bacterium that converts hydrogen into the heavier gas. Overall, front and back, about 6 percent of a cow's diet is lost as methane into the air.

Iowa Senator Charles E. Grassley suggested a dozen years ago that all cows should be fitted with anal airbags, complete with catalytic (or cattle-itic) converters, to harness this source of energy. But like everyone else, he was looking at the wrong end. Grassley also suggested that "if that does not work in reducing cow methane gas emissions, we can tax them. Call it another gas tax."

Well, that's exactly what politicians tried to do in New Zealand. According to a 2003 BBC report, New Zealand farmers were outraged by a proposed tax on the flatulence and belches coming from their sheep and cattle. This all came about when local scientists estimated that barnyard methane was responsible for more than half of the island country's greenhouse gases, prompting Prime Minister Helen Clark's government in Wellington to declare that a tax on ruminant farm animals would help the country meet its gas reduction quotas under the Kyoto Protocol on global warming.

Farts and belches from cows, sheep, goats, and deer, whose multiple stomachs are constantly digesting grasses, may account for only 15 percent of worldwide emissions of methane, but in countries with a large agricultural sector, the proportion is much higher. There are only about four million bipedal, single-stomach New Zealanders, but they own forty-five million sheep, ten million head of cattle, and many other animals, which produce 90 percent of their country's methane and 40 percent of their total greenhouse emissions. In June 2003, Patrick Goodenough, Pacific Rim Bureau Chief for CNSNews. com, reported that a herd of two hundred head of New Zealand dairy cattle produces enough annual methane gas to drive an average vehicle more than 120,000 miles.

The proposed "fart and belch" tax was expected to raise almost $5 million a year that could be used to fund research into ways of minimizing the effects of agricultural exhalations. However, members of a group called Federated Farmers of New Zealand nearly had a cow when they heard the news. They argued that since the government had signed the Kyoto agreement on behalf of every citizen, any taxes for research should be borne equally by all. The farmers were also baleful because the proposed levy would make it harder for them to compete against agricultural interests in countries that hadn't ratified Kyoto, including the United States and Australia.

Buoyed by a September 2003 opinion poll that said 80 percent of their fellow citizens opposed the tax, the Federated Farmers launched a campaign called Fight Against Ridiculous Taxes (FART). A thousand farmers descended on Wellington to stage rallies, collect petition signatures, and deliver a haymaker to Parliament. One farmer even drove his old tractor up the steps of the parliament building. Prime Minister Clark was besieged from all sides, especially the media, which kept coming up with snarky headlines like "Farmers Raise Stink Over Fart Tax" and "Flatulence Tax Just Government Hot Air." In late October, she backed off and decided to find other ways of meeting the country's Kyoto obligations. Federated Farmers Vice President Charlie Pedersen announced triumphantly that "farmers will be relieved that the government looks to have finally got the fart tax out of its system."

Meanwhile, all those cows keep belching. And farting.

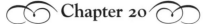

Chapter 20

A COUPLE OF
HOLLYWOOD STINKERS

It's no secret to anyone that Hollywood comedy writers have been coasting on fart gags for twenty-five years now. Young people—especially young guys—are the ones most likely to revisit a movie again and again if they love it, and nothing makes them come back for more like the lingering effects of jokes about farting and crapping in their pants.

So it was no surprise a few years ago that two different low-budget movies called *Fart* came out a few months apart from each other. Actually, one was *Fart: The Movie* (late 2001) and the other was *F.A.R.T. The Movie* (early 2002), and they both went straight to video.

Fart: The Movie was an hour-and-a-half flick directed by a forty-nine-year-old former network news cameraman named Ray Etheridge. It's the story of Russell (Joel Weiss), a guy who loves watching television, farting, and his girlfriend Heather (Shannandoah Sorin, who will someday create real problems if she ever becomes a marquee name). Heather is the complication here because she hates it when Russell farts, probably because she knows that if it comes down to a choice between his farts and her, she'll get blown out the door. She's also afraid, she tells him, that "if they ever allow farting on television, you'll never leave the house!" That evening he dozes off in front of the TV, and suddenly everything on the tube is related to flatulence: sitcoms, dramas, commercials, even the news—and here's where Etheridge's stable of unknown actors gets to shine. Did I say *unknown* actors? Well, there is one veteran some of you will recognize: an aging Conrad Brooks, who sleepwalked through a couple of 1950s Ed Wood movies, including *Plan 9 from Outer Space.*

F.A.R.T. The Movie is a little less honest than *Fart: The Movie* in its treatment of breaking wind. Written and directed by Matt Berman, it was originally released theatrically in 2000 under the name *Artie,* starring Seth Walther as an aging frat boy at Buck U. who goes into a fit of gastrointestinal distress every time he gets nervous or excited—a condition that complicates his campus love life.

In the very first scene, a flashback showing baby Artie just after delivery, he lets off a series of meconium-fueled noises, prompting the doctor to tell his parents, "Your son is a farter." At this point, you may already be complaining that since newborns can't fart until they've accumulated enough bacteria in their intestines, this first scene has destroyed your suspension of disbelief. Maybe if the baby had been just a couple of days older, you'd have bought the movie's premise hook, line, and stinker.

Having never seen the original *Artie,* I can't say for certain that this opener was part of the brief theatrical run, but I suspect that it was shot by the distributor that picked up the movie a year and a half later for DVD release, in order to accentuate Artie's problem. That would fit with the company's attempt to transform a tame *Animal House* or *Tommy Boy* wannabe into a butt-bang fiesta. First was the title change from *Artie* to *F.A.R.T. The Movie,* even though Artie's farting never affects the direction of the story or gets him into (or out of) real trouble. The new cover art was a red Whoopee Cushion, and the new taglines were "It's a real stinker!"—a rare flash of critical honesty—and "This movie is a gas!" Seth Walther's name was relegated to small print and the spotlight moved to "The Farley Brothers," Kevin and James (brothers of the late, lamented comic Chris Farley, star of *Tommy Boy*), even though they were second and third bananas with little appeal.

Devon Berube, a self-appointed critic from New Hampshire, said it best in his Internet Movie Database (http://imdb.com) review: "Basically this is a really bad college movie that attempts to use fart jokes to staple everything together. . . . It's like someone threw a bunch of ideas into the air and filmed the ones that landed in the circle on the floor." Another contributing voice, Cameron Scharnberg from Adelaide, Australia, was equally unimpressed: "This movie is an absolute pile of crap. . . . I didn't laugh once, which doesn't happen very often because I have a pretty immature sense of humour." And a reviewer named Chinpokêmon complained because "*F.A.R.T. The Movie* does not meet with the fart joke quota one would expect from both the movie's title and premise. It instead is a tame romantic comedy with a few fart jokes thrown in."

So what prompted Spectrum Films of Mesa, Arizona, to repackage a bad frat house romp as an even worse fart frolic? Could it have been simply "farts for farts' sake"? In a *Los Angeles Times* feature that ran on September 10, 2000, film director Reginald Hudlin (half of the Hudlin Brothers, known best for their *House Party* movies) announced that flatulence was still the funniest thing in Hollywood. "Broad comedy is safer because there's a greater margin for error," he said. "Even bad fart jokes get a chuckle."

Only a couple of weeks earlier, *Variety* editor Peter Bart had written, "Today, there's growing evidence that the fart jokes are driving out legitimate comedy."

And earlier that year, at the seventy-second Academy Awards ceremonies on March 27, the event's producer, Richard Zanuck, got ABC's approval for comic Robin Williams to sing the word "fart" when he performed an Oscar-nominated song, "Blame Canada," from the film *South Park: Bigger, Longer & Uncut*.

Given all that, why not green-light movies like *F.A.R.T. The Movie* and *Fart: The Movie*?

An old Jewish expression says you can't shine shit. You can't shine farts either—but that won't stop Hollywood from trying.

∽ Chapter 21 ∽

FEETS, DON'T FART AT ME NOW!

In my chapter on Hollywood ("Gone with the Wind") in *Who Cut the Cheese?* I credited Mel Brooks's 1974 Western parody, *Blazing Saddles*, with being the first mainstream American film with a fart joke. But after revisiting Jerry Lewis's *The Nutty Professor* from 1963, I have to revise my cinematic history. In one scene, as Lewis's title character, nerdy Julius Kelp, sneaks into a college lab, his shoes seem to be making suction noises on the tile floor that sound like wet farts. To avoid discovery he takes them off, but as he continues to tiptoe forward in his socks, you can still hear those crepe-sole crepitations, prompting Lewis to give the camera a dumbfounded double take. (Before we declare Lewis *le comique genius*, however, let me remind you that England's famous *Goon Show* comedian, Spike Milligan, used this same gag in a British film called *Postman's Knock* a year earlier.)

Anyway, four decades later, life imitated art, sort of, when Goosebumps Products—an insole manufacturer in Longwood, Florida, whose slogan is "Changing the way the world walks"— discovered that its famous Easy-Flo Gel insole, which normally "massages the foot with each step," was suddenly sounding like a farting contest. "They were Whoopee Cushions for the feet," Goosebumps executive Bryan Thomas told the *Orlando Sentinel* in early 2005. "It very nearly put us out of business." Goosebumps had to throw away at least 35,000 of its molded orthotic shoe inserts at a loss of over $200,000.

Goosebumps brought in chemist Richard Cavestri to find out what was causing the problem. Cavestri traced it back to eight drums of glycerin that Bell Chem, a local outfit, delivered to Goosebumps in late 2002 and early 2003. Though Goosebumps's contract called for a food-grade glycerin ideal for feet cushions, Bell Chem delivered a lower-grade variety that might also have been watered down. As a result, air bubbles formed inside the gel. And when buyers later slipped the insoles into their shoes and went stepping out, their feet made "a flatulence-like noise," according to Cavestri.

Bell Chem President John Cervo claimed he didn't know about the lawsuit until the *Sentinel* called him for a comment. "This is unbelievable," he said, insisting that the dispute was a private matter between Goosebumps and his insurance company, which will probably end up footing the bill. He referred any further questions to an attorney, who did not return phone calls. That's probably the best thing to do when you've been caught flat- and flatulent-footed.

Chapter 22

RUNNING WITH
THE WIND AT HIS BACK

In horse racing lore, they are thoroughbred names that will live forever: Man of War, Seabiscuit, Secretariat, Hoof Hearted . . . Hoof Hearted??

You can see him coming up on the outside in the stretch and crossing the finish line on countless sports-blooper TV shows like WB's *Most Outrageous Outtakes,* or the 2003 ABC special *ESPN's Blunderful World of Sports,* as the track announcer screams, "Hoof Hearted is taking the lead, he's pulling away, it's Hoof Hearted, Hoof Hearted, Hoof Hearted!"

Viewers all over America looked at each other and asked, "Did he just say what I think he said?"

Apparently there have been several Hoof Hearted thoroughbreds over the past quarter century. One reportedly raced in South Africa several decades ago; there was also one in Canada in the early 1990s, and another in California in 1982. In the late '90s, Hoof Hard Ed ran in the Midwest. Any one of those horses could be the one in the often-aired TV clip.

But the champion among the bunch is Sky Hoof Hearted, a four-year-old California gelding that in 2005 won several races around the Southwest, from Santa Anita (near Pasadena) to Turf Paradise (Phoenix). According to the Thoroughbred Database at www .pedigreequery.com, Sky Hoof Hearted is descended from Native Dancer—horse racing's first television star, who won everything in

1953 except the Kentucky Derby—through both his sire (Bertrando) and dam (Specific Gravity). He was bred by Martin J. Wygod and trained by F. C. Frazier at River Edge Farm, just outside Solvang.

So why would anybody name an expensive thoroughbred Hoof Hearted? Well, some people simply like to put one over on everybody with a practical joke, especially when there's a gatekeeper of good taste, which in this case is the all-powerful Jockey Club. Thoroughbreds have to be registered with the Jockey Club within a year of their birth (they're all given an official birthday of January 1 of the year they're born to put them into an age group for racing) and named by the February of the year they turn two. The owners submit six names in order of preference for the Jockey Club's approval, and there are rules for what names can't be used, including "names that are suggestive or have a vulgar or obscene meaning," according to racing expert Cindy Pierson Dulay—"Names considered in poor taste."

Like Hoof Hearted.

Since a horse's name can't be changed after its first professional race, some owners try to sneak sly, innocent-looking monikers past the Jockey Club judges, before the track announcers rattle them off over the loudspeakers. By then, the horse is out of the barn, with his name intact. Along with Peony's Envy, there have been Nip Pulls, Potopein, and If You See Kay. More subtle was the name of a 1979 filly, Breakwind, sired by Warm Breeze.

But none of them has gained the legendary stature of Hoof Hearted. In my mind's eye, I can see that proud fellow at full gallop, flared nostrils steaming, as the announcer yells, "Hoof Hearted is rounding the bend and coming up the rear!" And yes, of course he wins by a nose.

\text{Chapter 23}

Chapter 23

PULL MY FIN

In the 1973 novel *Breakfast of Champions*, Kurt Vonnegut's fictional science fiction writer, Kilgore Trout, came up with an alien race called the Tralfamadorians, who communicated by tap dancing and farting. Far-fetched? Well, maybe the tap dancing. But right here on earth we have nonfictional creatures who use flatulence as a kind of primitive language—and no, I'm not talking about twelve-year-old boys.

For example, in the August 2000 issue of *Discovery* magazine, writer Josie Glausiusz observed that the deadly Sonoran coral snake and the western hook-nosed snake—both natives of the American Southwest—have an odd way of scaring off predators. "When threatened," she wrote, "they emit rumbling air bubbles from the cloaca, the common opening for sex and excretion at a snake's rear end." Both types of snake have muscles that can form pockets of compressed air and then release them in loud pops. Bruce Young, an experimental morphologist at Lafayette College in Easton, Pennsylvania, told Glausiusz, "Essentially it's snake flatulence."

A couple of years later, in another realm altogether, Dr. Ben Wilson, marine biologist at the University of British Columbia's Bamfield Marine Science Centre, heard a strange noise emanating from his lab's herring aquarium one evening. "At first, I thought someone was hiding in the cupboard pulling a prank," he said later. Turning up the volume of the fish tank microphone, he heard what sounded like farts, accompanied by tiny air bubbles coming from the rear ends of several herring.

Intrigued by this phenomenon, Dr. Wilson picked up the telephone and enlisted the help of Robert Batty, senior research scientist at the Scottish Association for Marine Science in Oban, Scotland. While Wilson studied Pacific herring caught in British Columbia, Batty focused on Atlantic herring from the British seacoast. The fish were placed into laboratory tanks where they could be studied with hydrophones and infrared video cameras. Sure enough, whether Canadian or British, the herring farted in high-frequency bursts up to twenty-two kilohertz, accompanied always by streams of bubbles. At times, the tanks resembled old Lawrence Welk TV shows, and the fish didn't seem to be the least bit embarrassed about it, because there wasn't a red herring in the bunch.

"It sounds very much like someone blowing a high-pitched raspberry," Batty told James Owen in the November 10, 2003, edition of *National Geographic News.* At first, Batty and Wilson suspected that the herring used their depth charges to frighten off predators, or for buoyancy, like the sand tiger shark that gulps air at the water's surface, swallows it into its stomach, and farts out whatever is required for it to maintain its depth under water.

The herring were in fact gulping air at the surface like sand tiger sharks and storing it in their swim bladder, not using stomach gas from food digestion. But Drs. Batty and Wilson determined that the herring were releasing air bubbles not for buoyancy but rather as a way of maintaining contact with each other after dark without giving away their positions to predatory fish, whose hearing is less acute.

This "water-breaking" seemed like one of those discoveries that could elevate a mere researcher into a respected, perhaps even famous scientist, but when Ben Wilson sat down to prepare an article for the prestigious British scientific journal *Biology Letters,* he had a problem. How do you describe farting fish "without sounding too silly," as he put it later? The secret lay in scientific-sounding euphemisms.

Fish farts? Too colloquial, not to mention vulgar.

Piscine poots? Not serious enough.

Ichthyological butt bubbles? Even sillier.

So Wilson limited himself to terms like "burst pulse sounds," "digestive system venting," and "bubble expulsion from the anal duct region." As for a formal designation that such a natural occurrence required in the scientific community, he settled on *fast repetitive tick* (FRT).

Wilson's explanation that FRTs were simply a kind of Morse code between fish prompted the *Miami Herald*'s nationally known columnist/humorist Dave Barry to ask what these herring might have been discussing. "I mean, we're talking about creatures with roughly the same IQ as a Tic Tac," he wrote. "They are not down there discussing Marcel Proust. My guess is they're probably breaking wind to convey extremely simple messages such as: 'Hey, it's dark!' 'I know! The same thing happened last night!'"

Barry contacted Dr. Wilson to ask if those FRT-ing herring were males, since it's a well-known scientific fact that human males break wind purely for the sense of accomplishment it gives them. But when Dr. Wilson told him that it was difficult to tell male and female herring apart, Barry suddenly envisioned a whole new explanation:

"Maybe that's what they're communicating about: 'Hey, you want to mate?'

"'Sure! My name is Bob!'

"'Hey, my name is Bob, too!'

"'Uh-oh!'"

(If you'd like to hear a herring fart, check out www.zoology.ubc.ca/~bwilson/herring.htm.)

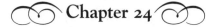

Chapter 24

WHEN IS A FART INDECENT?

The historic day was February 3, 2005. No, I'm not talking about the forty-sixth anniversary of Buddy Holly's plane crash. The event in question has even deeper implications—a new line in radio censorship was crossed. Shock jock Howard Stern was told by his corporate bosses that because of new FCC guidelines, the farts on his nationally syndicated show were too long and too wet.

That's not exactly what the FCC said, but with today's arbitrary standards of government censorship, not to mention stiff fines, the bosses at radio station WXRK-FM in Manhattan weren't taking any chances.

It began when Stern was talking to a very attractive young schoolteacher about her lesbian trysts. When she mentioned that she was living with her parents because she couldn't afford her own place, Stern offered her $500 if she would let another guest, Will the Farter, a young guy capable of farting at will, poot into her face five hundred times. She reluctantly agreed, and Will did his nasty business in different positions—lying on his back with his feet in the air, kneeling on all fours, etc.—as she kept her eyes clenched tight and her nose close to his butt.

After the segment ended and Stern moved on to other business, his producer, Gary Dell'Abate, came into the studio to tell him that the station manager, Tom Chiusano, had been going crazy during the rectal volley and used the seven-second delay button to "dump" many of the farts off the air. An occasional fart was apparently okay, but when they got too lengthy or sounded too moist and soggy, Chiusano felt he had to edit them out. "Howard said that was absolutely crazy and there is no FCC rule against farting," according to Stern's web page (http://howardstern.com). "Farting is second-grade humor!" He went into a rant, begging to be free of his contract with media conglomerate Infinity Broadcasting Corp. because he couldn't take being censored anymore. (At this point, Stern had already announced that when his contract with Infinity expired at the end of 2005, he would be moving to Sirius Satellite Radio, where the FCC has no jurisdiction.) To make matters worse, Dell'Abate reported that he had also received a list from Chiusano about old comedy bits they could no longer rebroadcast during their *Best of Stern* shows, thanks to recent FCC pressure. Stern read the list of no-nos on the air. One of the banned bits was him talking about having an "anal fissure."

The next day, when a listener rang Stern's program to find out why Will's farts had been so heavily edited, Stern took the opportunity to explain that Chiusano had been discussing the proper length and dampness of farts off the air for several days, before the topic came up on air. To paraphrase the late Supreme Court Justice Potter Stewart, Chiusano didn't know what a too-long or too-wet fart was, but he knew it when he heard it. "He's our own personal Fart Guard," Stern said, adding that the whole idea was ridiculous because the FCC had never fined anyone for airing farts before, and even if they tried to levy a fine, the station could take them to court, which would be hilarious because then the bureaucrats and politicians would have to elucidate for the record what a proper fart should sound like.

But the real problem, Stern lamented, was that the FCC would never allow the matter to go to court. In the past, when radio executives tried to stand up against unreasonable FCC rules or decisions, the federal agency had put their various station acquisitions and license renewals into legal limbo. "It's extortion," Stern complained, "but somehow our government is allowed to do it legally." In the meantime, he said, even though Chiusano had recently knocked Will the Farter's record-setting thirty-second blast off the air (see chapter 45), anyone interested could still hear it on the Howard Stern website.

Two weeks later, on February 17, Chiusano officially told Stern that he could no longer do "extended farting" on the show, whatever that meant. Stern insisted that he wanted to fart, it was his show, and he found farts just as funny now as he did when he was five. "My whole life, all I ever wanted to do was fart in a microphone," he said. He promised that as soon as he left terrestrial radio for Sirius, he would return to the old fart jokes and bits he used to do.

A month later, on March 14, the topic came up again when Stern wanted to bring Will the Farter back on the show to celebrate his upcoming marriage. Unfortunately, Tom Chiusano wouldn't allow them to do any comedy bits with Will, because his farts, being spontaneous, couldn't be monitored for length or wetness ahead of time. When Will announced over the phone that he'd like to bring in a friend who didn't mind being farted on, he was told that Chiusano wouldn't let that happen either, because the new station rules barred anyone from farting on or at another person.

Naturally, Stern fans had a field day with all this nonsense, but former TV critic Jeff Jarvis at BuzzMachine (http://buzzmachine .com) probably blogged it best:

> Howard Stern got a new ruling from the lawyers this morning: No long farts. Short farts are okay. Fart sounds made with the mouth (or, I assume, armpit) are apparently okay. But long farts from the fart factory are now feared to be illegal. . . .
>
> I picture a conference table. Around the table are five lawyers, each dressed in a very, very expensive dark suit. On the table is a small tape recorder.
>
> A paralegal presses the "play" button.
>
> "BRRRRRRPPPPPPPPPTTTTTTTTT!!!"
>
> "Too long," says the first lawyer.
>
> "I agree," says a second lawyer.
>
> And so forth. I imagine that these five lawyers spend an entire workday assessing a multitude of fart sounds. Two weeks later, Viacom [Infinity's parent company] receives a bill for $15,000 for "broken wind assessment."

There's poetic justice in there somewhere.

To appreciate the significance of Howard Stern's being silenced (or at least muffled), you have to know that for the past twenty-five years he's been on the media's cutting-cheese edge, farting regularly into his microphone, hosting farting contests, and playing a superhero named Fartman (see the "Adventures of Fartman" chapter in *Who Cut the Cheese?*). "Fartman just flew in from the [West] Coast, and boy is his ass tired," Stern announced at one point in 1996, when it looked like New Line Cinema would be green-lighting a Fartman movie. But Stern, who bought the full rights to the Fartman character in 1986 from its National Lampoon creators, backed out when New Line insisted on a G-rated script. Since then, Fartman's thunder has been stolen by a character in the 1999 film *Mystery Men* named Spleen (played by Paul Reubens, better known as Pee Wee Herman), whose power was his ability to discharge farts so lethally putrid that they incapacitated anyone within noseshot. So naturally Stern was in no mood to see the rest of his butt-cracking legacy disappear.

In early October 2005, with less than three months to go before his Infinity contract ended, Stern delivered a parting shot to the FCC by staging an all-day fartathon on his new Sirius Satellite radio band, Channel 100, to underscore just how much the agency had crippled terrestrial radio. The show's concept had begun a week earlier when a listener called in to report that Channel 100's scroll screen on his Sirius system read: "We're building toward Howard's arrival in January." Stern started riffing about how executives at Sirius wanted him to put up some kind of programming right away, even if it was just a tone, so that people would know their Sirius radios were working. Another caller suggested that Stern should introduce his channel by playing a tape of nonstop farting. Stern sidekick Artie Lange took the idea a step further by suggesting that Stern get live farters to work around the clock, which prompted Gary Dell'Abate to report that the program's semi-professional farters, who had been out of commission since the FCC crackdown, were dying to go back to work and get crackin'.

So the pooting stalwarts—Will the Farter, Junior the Farter, Dan the Farter, and Debbie the Queefer (who makes noises with the muscles of her vagina)—were quickly rounded up, and Sirius was instructed to change the scrolls on Channel 100 to "Farters coming soon." The result was one full day of live farting, unrestrained by any restrictions beyond pure talent, as the Flatulent Four worked in six-hour shifts. At the end of twenty-four hours, the channel returned to silence, but Stern had made his point.

Though none of the butt fluttering could be simulcasted or rebroadcasted on Stern's syndicated radio show, it was the main topic for days, as dozens of listeners called in to rave about what "great radio" awaited everyone in the sky, far above the reach of the FCC.

At the end of 2005, when Howard Stern finally abandoned earth-bound radio, he left open the question of what kind of fart, if any, the FCC would tolerate on the nation's airwaves from here on. With Stern gone, it's unlikely that anyone will be bold enough to push the envelope . . . or pull anyone's finger too strenuously, lest the fart go on for a second too long.

Chapter 25

WAR STINKS . . .
AND IT'S GETTING STINKIER!

A former Pentagon scientist has been working on weaponizing the fart for modern warfare and domestic crowd control, according to a November 2002 article in the *Los Angeles Times.* Actually, the idea's not entirely new. During World War II, Division 19, a secret psychological operations department within the Office of Special Services (OSS, America's pre-CIA spy outfit), developed a fecal-smelling mixture packed in a squirt tube, and called it Who Me? The sulfur-based substance smelled roughly like the odor that's added to natural gas to make it noticeable, with a dose of spoiled mushrooms mixed in. The OSS shipped tubes of the stinky stuff to occupied China and distributed them to children, who then sneaked up behind Japanese officers on crowded streets and squirted the liquid on the seats of their pants. Because of their exaggerated sense of personal dignity—called "face"—the Japanese were deeply humiliated when people around them thought they had farted or shit in their pants. The compound's name, incidentally, was based on the fact that the gesture among Japanese for "Who, me?" was pointing a finger at the nose, rather than at the chest as Americans do.

Today, Pamela Dalton, a cognitive psychologist at the Monell Chemical Senses Center in Philadelphia, is working with the Pentagon's Nonlethal Weapons Program to combine Who Me? with another fetid formula called U.S. Government Standard Bathroom Malodor, which bathroom cleanser and deodorizer manufacturers originally invented to test the effectiveness of their products. (In other words, Bathroom Malodor had to be more repugnant than anything that might appear naturally in or around somebody's toilet bowl— maybe even bad enough to knock a fly off a turd.) During Bathroom Malodor's sniff trials, people of various ethnic backgrounds called it the vilest stench that had ever assaulted their olfactories. Even Ms. Dalton had to admit that Bathroom Malodor "smells like shit, but much, much stronger. It fills your head. It gets you in ways that are unimaginable. It's not something you are likely to come across in the real world."

Mixing what she called "the worst of Bathroom Malodor and Who Me?" Dalton came up with Stench Soup, a miasma so execrable and obnoxious that it practically freezes people in their tracks, clouds their minds, and creates fear and loathing by activating the brain's primitive responses to nasty and dangerous smells that allowed our ancestors to run away and survive. If you've been gang-sprayed by a mother skunk and all of her brood, or if you've had to take a crap in an overloaded Porta-Potti on a 105°F day, you may have an inkling of what it feels like to get a blast of Stench Soup.

So far, the Pentagon hasn't figured out how to weaponize Dalton's synthetic fart into what writer Stephanie Pain of *New Scientist* magazine calls "the mother of all stink bombs." There is also a problem of whether Stench Soup could be considered a toxic chemical weapon, subject to ethical and legal tests mandated by the international Chemical Weapons Convention.

But if it ever passes muster, a Stench Soup warhead could probably replace the infamous Daisy Cutter, the massive firebomb that U.S. planes used against dug-in Taliban and Al Qaida fighters during the Afghanistan war. We could call it the Cheese Cutter.

Chapter 26

MEET THE DUMFARTS

How would you like to spend your whole life telling people, "Yes, I'm a Dumfart"?

Actually, you'd more likely be telling them, "Ja, ich bin ein Dumfart," because Dumfarts are most plentiful in the heartland of Austria, with a few strays in Germany. Linz, Austria, seems to be their ancestral home; many Dumfarts live there, including the owner of the Dumfart Gas-und Wasserleitung Installationsgesellschaft, which installs plumbing and gas lines. They're rare in the United States and England, most likely because any immigrant Dumfarts changed their name as soon as they realized why everybody was guffawing.

Anyway, besides concert tuba player Karl Dumfart (savor for a moment the image of a Dumfart tooting the tuba), the most famous Dumfarts are Josef and Maria, who gained posthumous renown when a photo of their grave marker in Austria made the rounds on the Internet.

Among the many websites celebrating the Dumfart couple is Louisville Mojo (http://louisvillemojo.com), which asks visitors to supply a caption to the photo. Among the submissions:

"In today's news, the man who invented the pull-my-finger joke died at the age of 97."

"Josef and Maria Dumfart are survived by their only child, Ima Dumfart."

"Their presence will linger on with us for years to come."

According to Manfred Dumfart, an Austrian engineer who is presently working in Johannesburg, South Africa, Maria was his mother and Josef was either her father or grandfather. "The whole Dumfart family tree is not 100 percent clear to me, but my 'uncle' in Austria should know more about it," he said in a March 2005 email. "I will contact him, because I want to know myself more about our family."

Since then, Herr Dumfart has apparently caught wind of what I was doing. I'm still waiting to hear back from him.

Chapter 27

KIRK TO SPOCK: MIND-MELD *THIS!*

In 2001, actor William Shatner videotaped an easygoing conversation between himself and former costar Leonard Nimoy about how the 1960s *Star Trek* TV series and subsequent movie franchise affected their lives and careers. Shatner then packaged it as a seventy-five-minute documentary called *Mind Meld: Secrets Behind the Voyage of a Lifetime* (Creative Light Home Video)—a reference to the ability of Nimoy's Vulcan character, Mr. Spock, to create a telepathic empathy with other creatures.

In the movie, after sitting around and talking in the garden, the two old friends adjourned to Nimoy's memorabilia-stuffed library. While Shatner was adjusting himself in his chair in mid-conversation, it looked and sounded as if he'd let off a butt-cheek sneak that turned out to be not very sneaky. Either that or somebody stepped on a Tribble. Apparently neither the actors nor the crew noticed it at the time (perhaps Shatner had put his sphincter phaser on *stun*), but when the enterprising Shatner released the *Mind Meld* tape on his website (http://williamshatner.com), the fart instantly reverberated throughout the Trekkie galaxy like a supernova. When Howard Stern began playing it on his radio show, the squeak became an underground media star. "The morning zoo buzz is quickly rivaling the adolescent tittering spawned by *Girls Gone Wild*," said film reviewer G. Noel Gross at DVD Talk (http://dvdtalk.com). "Not since the Zapruder film [of JFK's assassination] has a stretch of footage been more scrutinized. Cap'n Kirk is yammering about why the crew [of *Star Trek*] hates his stinky guts when at along about timecode 52:47 the offending audio manifests. It's by far the more pronounced of what some theorists have speculated to be as many as seven gassy releases."

So, did Shatner vulcanize the air with sulfur?

Did James T. Kirk launch a photon torpedo at his first officer?

On November 13, 2001, when Shatner visited Stern's program to promote some of the crap he's endlessly flogging (in this case, a competitive cooking show), the shock jock asked him about the illusory fart. Shatner insisted that he didn't do it. The sound man, he claimed, had moved a boom microphone at just the moment he squirmed in his chair.

On the following night, during an appearance on NBC's *Late Night with Conan O'Brien*, Shatner had to defend himself again.

By mid-2004, it looked as if that flatulent fillip (or imaginative figment thereof) had faded from public memory—but then along came a new *Star Trek* Collector's Edition DVD that included *Mind Meld* as a bonus, and the controversy began anew. It threatens to cling on forever in our cultural memory.

Meanwhile, since all radio transmissions go off into deep space, Shatner's butt squib is now heading for Epsilon IV, where no fart has gone before, and probably will not arrive until, say, four hundred light years from now. Unless, of course, it hits warp speed.

Chapter 28

THE SWEET SMELL OF SUCCESS

It was a "eureka" moment in the life of Steve Schuster. Or better yet, a "you reek" moment. Just before getting on an airplane, he decided to take a last-minute pee in the airport men's room to avoid having to use the cramped, onboard facilities. But when he walked in, "I was hit immediately with the unmistakable stink of fresh poop," he says. "Bad enough that my eyes actually started watering."

We've all suffered through this torment at public toilets. Somebody's crap stinks bad enough to make the mirrors shimmer, and all you can do is hold your breath, do your business as quickly as possible, and get the hell out of there. But Steve is a guy who needs to fix things. "My dad told me to always leave the campsite better than I found it," says the former engineer, who now runs his own Massachusetts-based marketing firm for high-tech companies. "So when I got a whiff of that smell, I told myself, 'This doesn't have to be. Why should poop stink like that?' But instead of spraying something to cover it up or trying to suck it away with a ventilating fan, I thought, 'Why not go to the source?'"

In other words, find out what creates such a stench. Schuster wasn't concerned about his own poop so much, because we all know that our own shit and farts don't stink all that badly. He was more concerned about changing everyone else's, so that if he ever had to go into another public bathroom, he wouldn't be assaulted like that again. On a more altruistic level, it would be a global mission of making the world smell just a little bit better. Kind of like lighting one little candle and making things brighter—or at least a little bluer, what with all that methane gas. But Schuster needed a rallying cry to rouse the masses. That's when the words "Take a Whiff!" popped into his head.

Five years later he came up with an antistink pill called, you guessed it, Whiff!—complete with exclamation point (see http://takeawhiff.com for more info).

"Most of us use underarm deodorant, not because we're offended by our own odor, but because we worry about offending other people," says Schuster. "It's simple courtesy. So why not deodorize our poop and our farts, too?" Yes, farts, because according to Schuster, "Whiff!'s odor-reducing mechanisms are related to gas and have the same odor-mitigating effect on farts as on poop. I can verify this from several years of usage. Whiff! does not reduce the volume of gas, just the odor."

Though some people's body chemistry may contribute to really stinky poop, the main problem is diet. If you eat a greasy cheeseburger with onions, or a 7-Eleven burrito, and wash it all down with beer, whoa, your shit's gonna stink like Jersey City. Much of our modern diet is processed food, complete with sodium and additives whose job is to ensure longer shelf life by killing anything else that eats it before you do—and by the time the bacteria in your stomach have adapted to it, they have mutated and evolved into superpredators. With Whiff! Schuster wanted to add something naturally "sweet" to the stomach—kind of like freshening the breath with parsley— and mitigate the creation of toxic fumes. He claims that Whiff!'s ingredients are all natural. First there's FOS, a natural sugar extracted from Jerusalem artichoke (a northern United States tuber that's not really an artichoke, but rather in the same family as the sunflower). Native Americans have used Jerusalem artichoke as a food staple for centuries. According to Schuster, FOS promotes the growth of "friendly" bifidobacteria and lactobacilli, "known to reduce the amount of pathogenic—'unfriendly'—bacteria in the colon." Then there's chlorophyll extracted from alfalfa; and desert yucca, a cactus. Taken in capsule form, Whiff! is supposed to create a healthier environment—"friendly flora"—in the mucous membrane of the large intestine. It begins working after about two weeks, the time it takes the body—with Whiff!'s help—to rid itself of the old, stinky bacteria. "Whiff! reduces poop odor across the board," claims Schuster, "but if you eat a lot of red meat, onions, or other smelly foods, your poop will still have some odor, just not as strong as before."

A month's supply of sixty capsules costs $15. Schuster asserts that the laboratory that manufactures Whiff! capsules follows guidelines set forth in U.S. Food and Drug Administration (FDA) regulations, although the product is not FDA-approved. "The approval process costs about $100,000. That's why I'm obliged to put the same FDA disclaimer in there that all nutritional supplements must use."

In other words, Whiff! could be just a poop-sweetening, fart-freshening placebo that only makes you *think* you don't stink so bad anymore.

In late 2005, Steve Schuster was invited to visit the *Howard Stern* show, where the host immediately pointed out that he himself would never take Whiff! because the smell was part of the fun of taking a crap. In fact, Stern said he often held off flushing for a few minutes simply to savor the aroma wafting all around him. Sidekick Robin Quivers wondered if simply adopting a healthier lifestyle, with unprocessed foods, would have the same effect as taking the recommended dosage. When Stern asked how people could tell if the pills are working, Schuster said, "If it turns your stool a rich green, it's working. Green is good."

That prompted comic Artie Lange to comment that, if nothing else, Whiff! sounded like a great idea for St. Patrick's Day.

Chapter 29

OUR FARTS WERE HAPPY AND GAY!

According to an article in the *Redditch Advertiser* (an English newspaper) that ran on February 16, 2005, a Worcestershire politician named Tom Wareing got himself into hot water during Great Britain's Lesbian, Gay, Bisexual, and Transgender History Month when he compared homosexuals with people who either fart too heartily or can't shit worth a shit. That's not exactly how he said it, of course. The fart first hit the fan when the Crabbs Cross County councilman complained publicly that pro-gay organizations were brainwashing children by "perpetrat[ing] the myth that Shakespeare was homosexual and Florence Nightingale a lesbian." Annoyed that such groups might get public funding, Wareing told the local Resources and Cultural Services representative at a council meeting, "According to medical evidence, one in eight of the population suffers from constipation, while one in four suffers from flatulence, yet no local authority to date has provided funds . . . in order to celebrate such conditions, especially the various cadences that are possible in the act of breaking wind." So why, he reasoned, should the supposed 10 percent of the population that's gay be any different? In other words, why should taxpayer money be poured down a glory hole?

Just a couple of months later, in Sweden, researchers were studying whether gay men and straight men react differently to body odor, including, most likely, farts. Dr. Ivanka Savic Berglund, senior consultant neurologist at Stockholm's Karolinska Institute, wrote in the May 3, 2005, issue of the *Proceedings of the National Academy of Sciences* that when gay men were given PET scans (an imaging technique that reveals blood flow and neuron activity in the brain), the anterior hypothalamus region of their brains—which controls sexual behavior—became activated as they sniffed a testosterone-related chemical taken from male sweat. On the other hand, that same area of straight men's brains didn't react at all—until they took a whiff of an estrogen compound made from female urine. What one man considered an odor, another man took as a subliminal love potion. It was all a matter of sexual orientation.

Dr. Savic's research harkened back to a controversial 1991 report by California neurobiologist Dr. Simon LeVay, which held that a certain area of the hypothalamus is only half as large in women and gay men as it is in straight men—a conclusion that hints that gays can't help being who they are, no matter how many Evangel Society Bible classes they take. But more important, Dr. Savic's experiments showed that certain subtle human hormones that we sweat from our bodies—called pheromones—may have a more powerful effect on other people than previously thought, and that women and gay men react to the same pheromones, while straight men react to others. Since those little love molecules are produced inside our bodies, they are also sloughed off into our intestines and eventually end up steaming from our nether regions. I mentioned in chapter 7 that novelist James Joyce rhapsodized about how the scent of his wife's farts invigorated him. More than two hundred years earlier, Jonathan Swift recognized the same sexual excitement in his poem called *The Problem* (1699), when he wrote, "Love's fire, it seems, like inward heat, / Works in my Lord by stool and sweat, / Which brings a stink from ev'ry pore, / And from behind, and from before; / Yes, what is wonderful to tell it, / None but the fav'rite nymph can smell it."

As for Councilman Wareing back in England, well, maybe he was protesting too much. Maybe we should take a look at his hypothalamus.

Chapter 30

WHO CUT THE OLIGOSACCHARIDES?

In *Who Cut the Cheese?* I talked about the "flatulent factors," complex sugars called oligosaccharides (raffinose, stachyose, and verbacose) that exist in fairly high amounts in most green vegetables, legumes, and beans. Your average herbivore can break down these carbohydrates without even thinking about it, but we humans can't, so we pass them along through our digestive tract as a movable feast, a veritable smorgasbord, for our millions of bacterial guests, and the next thing you know, a cloud of gas is thundering down our lower intestine searching for a way out and refusing to take no for an answer.

Science has tried to defeat oligosaccharides by breeding a fartless (or less fartful) bean, and by prepackaging exotic bacterial cultures in products like Beano, which can be sprinkled or squirted on food, but both attempts have achieved only modest success. Old wives claim that soaking beans and legumes in water overnight can make them less gaseous, as long as they're not cooked in the same water. And now, according to a BBC report dated March 27, 2002, scientists at the Bhabha Atomic Research Centre in Trombay, India, claim that beans can be partly neutralized by blasting them with radioactive rays, just like something out of a fifties sci-fi movie.

Irradiation technology is already commonly used all over the world to extend the shelf life of fruits, herbs, and spices by killing the bacteria that make them rot, but this idea of making "the musical fruit" less musical could have a powerful effect on the world's diet, not to mention smog and global warming.

The Indian researchers broke mung beans, chickpeas, black-eyed peas, and red kidney beans into three separate groups. They zapped the first group with a low-intensity gamma-ray beam, and the second with a beam three times as strong. The third group wasn't irradiated at all. Then, adding a touch of "old wives" technology, all the beans were soaked in cold water for two days before being tested.

Jammala Machaiah, who carried out the research with colleague Mrinal Pednekar, wrote in the scientific journal *Food Chemistry* that the radiation treatment itself broke down the sugars only slightly. But when the beans and legumes were then soaked, their oligosaccharide levels dropped according to how much they had been nuked beforehand. For example, soaking low-dose-radiated mung beans reduced their oligosaccharide levels by 70 percent, whereas levels in high-dosed beans were cut by 80 percent. In beans that hadn't been irradiated, the soaking process dropped their fart-inducing properties only 35 percent. Black-eyed peas and chickpeas also showed a marked improvement with irradiation; but kidney beans, which have low levels of oligosaccharides to begin with, were unaffected.

Machaiah said, "In India, beans are a very popular and important part of the national diet, but some people can't eat a lot of beans because of the flatulence problem. This is unfortunate, as it is a very good source of essential nutrients. Irradiation would make beans less of a problem."

And not just for humans. Stephen Cole, technical director of Enzyme Services & Consultancy in Blackwood, Wales, is looking at new ways to break down oligosaccharides in animal feed to prevent pigs and chickens from becoming bloated and stinking up their sties and coops. He believes that oligosaccharides are "anti-nutritional factors. If irradiation helps reduce them, that's good."

Considering that our crowded world is getting even more crowded every day, anything we can do to reduce methane gas is a blessing to mankind. Also, vegetable diets are easier on the environment than meat-based diets, so anything that makes beans and veggies less gassy has to be good, right?

Well, Catherine Collins, spokeswoman for the British Dietetic Association, disagrees. She told *BBC News Online* that oligosaccharides are good for us because the bacteria that attack them maintain our natural defenses against other unpleasant intrusions. "The immune system is [kept] in a state of readiness," she said. "When it meets something [worse] like salmonella, it very quickly leaps into action and gets rid of it." She said that oligosaccharides also help control cholesterol levels.

Glenn Gibson, a food microbiologist at England's Reading University, is also against nuking the fart factors, but for another reason: "Flatulence is an important indicator of a healthy gut system. It's only a social problem. You need to expel gas to ensure your gut is functioning properly." In other words, whenever you blast off a good one, think of it as a toast to your good health.

I can think of a bigger problem. If we start eating irradiated beans on a regular basis, what happens if our farts go nuclear? They're explosive enough as it is.

Chapter 31

ROSES ARE RED,
FARTS ARE BLUE, BUT ONLY
IF YOU LIGHT THEM, TOO!

When *Who Cut the Cheese?* came out in 1999, only a couple of newspapers reviewed or even mentioned it, and none of them ventured near that four-letter F word that dare not speak its name behind your back in mixed company. But that all changed on June 18, 2004, when Mark Caro wrote a piece for the *Chicago Tribune* about how many of the new Father's Day cards were basically fart jokes:

"A couple are sitting up in bed, smiling at each other, beneath the printed words: 'On Father's Day, Dear, I just want you to know I love you.' Ah, a nice Father's Day card. Let's open it up:

"'. . . even if you do fart in bed.'

"Egads! Sorry, that had no business appearing in a family newspaper," Caro wrote. "Let's find another one."

Next up was a card with an innocent looking dog with a "Pffft!" coming from off to the side, where a cherished member of the family was about to put the blame on him.

[Authorial aside: Enough of this blaming-the-dog nonsense. Dammit, take responsibility for your own farts! Okay, now back to our regularly scheduled chapter.]

Still in Caro's pile of family cards were a "half dozen other ones that equate Dad with noxious fumes," he said, in preparation for his central question: "Okay, folks, who put the second 'r' into Father's Day?"

Cue the greeting card lady. "I think it's a safe way to be shocking," said Rachel Bolton, a spokeswoman for Hallmark, which maintains its Shoebox line of greeting cards that deviate from the venerable company's hoary homilies and feel-good felicitations. "It wouldn't appear on cards if it hadn't been part of virtually everyone's experience at one point in life."

At this juncture in the article [*self-promotion alert! self-promotion alert!*], Mark Caro phoned me for a comment, and since it's mine I'll use it here without fear of being called a plagiarist: "It seems like although farting has always been taboo, within families it's always a private joke," I told him. "'Pull my finger,' 'Is that a barking spider?'— this comes from parents dealing with their kids. Families hold these kind of things dear, whether they realize it or not. I think every family has one person that everybody else considers to be the farter."

Caro reasoned that that person had to be Dad, "unless I just missed the 'Pffft!' section of Mother's Day cards."

Indeed, American Greetings Corporation, which calls itself one of the world's largest makers of greeting cards, does sell more humorous cards around Father's Day than during any other time of the year, according to a spokeswoman. But it's hardly the only season or occasion for sending fart jokes to friends and loved ones. The only greeting card subsections at your local Wal-Mart or Hallmark shop not likely to have them are Weddings and Funerals.

Hey, wait a minute, I just thought of an idea for a sympathy card. A middle-aged gentleman is lying in his coffin during the viewing. His right forearm has been propped up, with the forefinger extended. The widow is speaking as she and another woman gaze down at him. When you open the card, it says, "He looks so natural."

Okay, here's another one that just popped into my head. A bride and groom are standing in front of a preacher. The groom's ready to put the ring on her finger, but with a smirk on her face she's holding out the wrong finger. Now open the card: "Yes, I do."

If any greeting card company out there plans on using either one, please send me a check. Or better yet, hire me. I need the work.

Anyway, the greeting card is a great year-round seller because it's the perfect format for a joke. On the front you get the setup. Then you open the card for the punch line. One, two, ba-*dum*!

For example, one recent card features a cartoon of a man saying, "I wanted to give you something really personal for your birthday." Inside: ". . . So I farted in this card."

Another card has a cartoon of a grinning cat saying, "I really hope you like this Valentine . . ." Inside: "Somebody farted in the card shop and I could only hold my breath long enough to grab this one!"

A cartoon of a reindeer with frost coming out of his mouth says, "If you can see your breath when it's cold outside . . ." Inside, the card says, ". . . How come you can't see your farts? Oh, well, Merry Christmas."

Above a cartoon of a dog with a shredded piece of paper in his mouth are the words "I originally bought you one of those neat, musical Easter cards that plays a song whenever you open it, but the dog ate it." Inside: "Now whenever he farts, he plays 'Easter Parade.'"

Some cards go far beyond the simple one-two. A cartoon skunk on the cover announces, "A poem for your birthday, 'All About Farts.'" Inside are ten pages of doggerel that end with, "We mustn't forget dear, sweet old farts like you!"

The apparent success of these cards demonstrates how casual we Americans have become over the past thirty years, not only about body humor but in our relationships with each other. But how much longer can this go on? Is the greeting card with a flatulent jibe destined to be an evergreen visitor whenever holidays and birthdays come around? Or will the jokes eventually run out of gas?

Chapter 32

LE PETOMANE—
FLATAL ATTRACTION

I s the world ready for Le Petomania?
Even though he's no longer here to blow his own trumpet, Joseph
Pujol, better known as Le Petomane, may be ready for his comeback. Who said his career was behind him? His career was *always*
behind him.

It's been over 110 years now since Pujol breezed into Belle Epoque
Paris and tickled funny bones on the Moulin Rouge's outdoor
Elephant stage, imitating birds, human voices, musical instruments,
and booming artillery with his talented tuchus. There was no other
entertainer like him. As actor Kelsey Grammer remarked to TV host
Jay Leno in 1995, "This man took the history books by the pages and
really ripped one out for himself."

Though Pujol's appellation has been translated sometimes as
"farting man," it actually means "fart mania"—a phenomenon that
could happen again. In addition to my own lengthy chapter on
him in *Who Cut the Cheese?* there are plenty of copies around of *Le
Petomane (1857–1945)*, the definitive biography by Jean Nohain and
F. Caradec (translated into English by British playwright Warren
Tute—yes, Tute), both Sherbourne Press's 1968 English language
originals and 1986 Random House reprints. Le Petomane also showed
up recently as a literary character, snuffing out candles and farting
"Clair de Lune" in Sarah Shun-lien Bynum's 2004 novel *Madeleine Is
Sleeping*—a fiction nominee for the prestigious National Book Award,

92

the literary world's Oscar. In a conversation with moderator David Medaris at a Madison, Wisconsin, book festival in September 2004, Bynum said, "In the course of haphazard reading or movie watching or music listening, I'd occasionally come across brief references to lives that would trouble or tickle me: the village idiot, the flatulent man, the woman singing the part of the leading man. I wouldn't do any further research; the one exception was Le Petomane, the farting artist, whose biography I read—a little novelty book found in the office of my father, who's a gastroenterologist."

But Le Petomane has found his greatest voice—orally and otherwise—in cinema, where a couple of actors have brought him to life. He made his first entrance in 1979, when Ian MacNaughton, the Scottish director who helmed most of the Monty Python Flying Circus movies, made a thirty-five-minute comedy called *Le Petomane* for British TV's innovative Channel 4. Casting the film, MacNaughton gave first crack at Le Petomane to Ron Moody, a London actor whom American audiences may recognize as the lead in Mel Brooks's early film *The Twelve Chairs* (1970). But Moody felt the part lacked a certain, oh, dignity and gravitas. So the director turned to Leonard Rossiter, the then-current star of one of Britain's favorite TV comedies, *The Rise and Fall of Reginald Perrin,* as well as a busy character actor who had appeared in a couple of Stanley Kubrick films, including *2001: A Space Odyssey.* Though the real Le Petomane was in his mid-thirties during his heyday at the Moulin Rouge, Rossiter was twenty years older and in some scenes had to be photographed carefully. *Le Petomane* followed the Nohain-Caradec biography, but comedy writers Ray Galton and Alan Simpson (who created British TV's *Steptoe and Son,* which became *Sanford and Son* in the United States) added a few gags of the sort that a good farter would play on the people around him, such as fooling a fellow soldier into thinking his boots were creaking as he walked. The film also suggested, despite a lack of any evidence, that Pujol made a recording of Debussey's "Clair de Lune"—perhaps that's where Sarah Shun-lien Bynum got the idea for Pujol's musical performance in *Madeleine Is Sleeping*—and that he ended his career after he began soiling himself onstage, the result of aging bowels. The farts in the film were created electronically by Electrophon Music, Ltd.

Four years later, in 1983, Ugo Tognazzi, age sixty-one, took over the part of Joseph Pujol in *Il Petomane* (released internationally as *Petomaniac*), a feature-length Italian production directed by Pasquale Festa Campanile. I must confess that I haven't seen this film, but I'm sure its basic message is that all things must pass. Unfortunately, that includes Rossiter and Tognazzi.

More recently, in 2001, Australian actor Keith Robinson was listed as portraying the al fresco fart man in Baz Luhrmann's overstuffed *Moulin Rouge,* but he was either left on the cheese-cutting-room floor or else he got lost in the film's loud and opulent emptiness.

Mel Brooks paid homage to Pujol in his 1974 breakthrough film *Blazing Saddles*—whose notorious cowboy campfire scene set the standard for Hollywood's flatulence excellence—by playing a character named Governor William J. LePetomane.

And then there's the mockumentary. An Albany, New York–based media artist named Igor Vamos and writer Bret Fetzer produced a fifty-six-minute film in 1998 called *Le Petomane: Fin de Siècle Fartiste* (End-of-the-Century Fartist), described by one critic as "a humorous deconstruction in the style of a PBS documentary." They resurrected and re-created Pujol using old photos and documents, newspaper clippings, archival footage (including clips of a Thomas Edison Company film of the 1900 Exposition Universelle in Paris and selections from the early films of the Lumière brothers and George Méliès), and a couple of scratchy, black-and-white reconstructions showing Le Petomane performing onstage (subverted by the actor's modern body language) and farting into a recording horn. There are also some deadpan talking heads: a doctor explaining how Pujol did his act; a great-grandson revealing family lore; and experts talking about Le Petomane's influence upon early filmmakers like Méliès, impressionist composer Erik Satie, various art movements of the early twentieth century, and the rise of modern industrialism. Unfortunately, Vamos is ham-handed in his juxtaposition of real and fake, and tone deaf when creating modern day interviewees. The only viewers likely to be fooled are those who are totally unfamiliar with Le Petomane and his *fin-de-siècle* milieu.

Currently, an independent filmmaker in Hollywood named Randolph Mack, who co-scripted *Burning Annie* (2003), says he has a Le Petomane project "in development." Mack admits he got the idea for the movie while reading my Pujol chapter in *Who Cut the Cheese?* "When I saw the item where Johnny Depp said that he'd love to play Le Petomane, I decided to write a screenplay." Depp is "interested" in the project, Mack claims, but the actor is withholding any commitment until he sees a final rewrite of the script.

The ideal director, of course, would be Depp's frequent collaborator, Tim Burton. Together, the two have already created a character named Edward who could cut the cheese or rip a good one with his scissor-like hands, and revived a 1950s figure, also named Ed, responsible for some of Hollywood's biggest stinkers. With a team like Depp and Burton, we could be fairly certain that their *Le Petomane* biopic wouldn't be just another blast from the past.

Chapter 33

CURING FARTS THE
OLD-FASHIONED WAY

Over the past four hundred years, pharmacologists, herbalists, and old wives have been prescribing green moss, ginger root, cloves, peppermint, rosemary, star anise (a licorice-flavored fruit), champagne, charcoal, and who knows what else to alleviate intestinal gas and cure flatulence. More recently, medical researchers suggest that the drug known generically as simethicone—marketed as Gas-X, Flatulex, Mylanta Gas Relief, and No-Fart (okay, I made up the No-Fart)—reduces intestinal bloating by decreasing the surface tension of gas bubbles.

But cocktail waitresses and bartenders claim they have the perfect low-cost antifart medicine. It's Angostura aromatic bitters, an herbal flavoring and stimulant that's been touted for more than a century as a digestive aid. Pharmacists, who prefer that you buy something pricier, won't mention Angostura bitters, but you can always find a four-ounce bottle for a few dollars at any neighborhood supermarket, usually near the margarita mix; and bartenders keep it on hand next to the grenadine and vermouth because it's an ingredient in several cocktails, including old-fashioneds (bourbon, a sugar cube, and bitters) and manhattans (whiskey, vermouth, and bitters). Cooks use it, too, for dosing sauces, salad dressings, soups, and just about anything else that needs a fillip.

The Angostura label suggests that one-to-four teaspoons after a meal will relieve gas. Nightclub workers say a mere teaspoon in a glass of a clear, carbonated liquid like club soda, 7-Up, or sparkling water will do the trick. Drink up and fart no more, at least for a while.

In 1824, in the Venezuelan port town of Angostura (renamed Ciudad Bolivar two decades later), Dr. J. G. B. Siegert developed Angostura bitters as a tonic to treat fatigue and stomach ailments. Siegert's blend—still a secret—reportedly contains over forty tropical herbs, plant extracts, and spices, including gentian root, which some researchers think is the prime ingredient for neutralizing farts. (Gentian plants are commonly used around the world as a remedy for various ailments, including high blood pressure, leprosy, snakebite, and venereal disease.) There are also "flavoring extracts and vegetable coloring material," not to mention a considerable amount of alcohol—40 percent by volume—which suggests that Angostura bitters has changed since its formula and trademark were taken over by Angostura International of Auburn, Maine, and held subject to U.S. FDA approval. (The bitters are still manufactured in Trinidad, West Indies, "By appointment to Her Majesty Queen Elizabeth II," according to the bottle's label.) There are other aromatic bitters, but only this one is called Angostura. Though it is, as doctor and nutritionist Andrew Weil described it, "essentially a tincture of gentian root"—much like an elixir in a suspiciously dark bottle once sold off the back of a medicine wagon—Angostura bitters is now the single most widely distributed bar item in the world.

In other words, it bars gas from roaring out of your ass like some raucous, drunken lout.

Chapter 34

THANK YOU FOR NOT FARTING

Almost thirty years ago, comic Steve Martin told a joke on his *Let's Get Small* album about a guy who sits down next to him in a bar and asks, "Mind if I smoke?"

"By equating farting with smoking tobacco on a popular comedy record (*Let's Get Small* was a top-ten hit on *Billboard*'s album chart in late 1977), Martin fired the first shot of the nascent anticigarette campaign that would eventually transform the United States from a hazy nation of "fag fiends" to a clear-sky country of nonsmokers.

And now that same message has come to mainstream television in the form of public service ads, like the following one.

The commercial shows a black family—parents and their three teenagers—in an SUV. Suddenly the kids start waving their hands, making gagging noises, and saying, "Roll down the window, oh my goodness!"

"That's foul, man!"

"Ah, you smell *that?*"

We've been led to believe that somebody blasted an insufferable sulfuric stinker—until Dad, behind the wheel, rolls down the window and tosses out his cigarette. A voice-over intones, "Don't pass gas, let it out."

A second ad shows a young family at home. The kids are complaining, "Man, is that you?" and "Grandpa, you're killing me over here!" The baby starts crying.

Again, a disembodied voice says, "Don't pass gas—take it outside. A smoke-free home is a lifesaver. And a money-saver."

Behind these public service announcements are the Ad Council, a prolific nonprofit producer of such ads, and the American Legacy Foundation, a Washington, D.C., nonprofit agency created after the tobacco industry and forty-five state attorneys general signed the November 1998 Master Settlement Agreement, which stipulated that part of the $206 billion settlement the industry owed the states had to be used for campaigns and programs to fight cigarette smoking. The foundation's message is that even if children can be persuaded not to smoke, they will still have a 25- to 40-percent greater risk of chronic respiratory problems, including asthma, if they're breathing their parents' secondhand smoke, "a toxic fog of gases including ammonia, carbon monoxide, and hydrogen cyanide." Hence the group's catchphrase, "Don't pass gas." (See http://dontpassgas.com for more information and the aforementioned commercials.)

The idea that smoking and stinking are noxious bedfellows has been around a while. *A New Dictionary of the Terms Ancient and Modern of the Canting Crew*, published in 1700, described "funk" as "Tobacco Smoak; also a strong Smell or Stink," and *A New Canting Dictionary* (1725) demonstrated the word thus: "What a Funk here is! What a thick Smoak of Tobacco is here! Here's a damn'd Funk, here's a great Stink!" The *Oxford English Dictionary* says that by the turn of the eighteenth century, *funk* was also being used as a verb meaning "to blow smoke upon" or "to cause an offensive smell."

In Scene 1, Act III, of his 1697 play, *The Provoked Wife*, dramatist John Vanbrugh (1664–1726) included the following exchange:

> LADY BRUTE: With all my heart, Belinda, don't you long to be married?
> BELINDA: Why, there are some things in it which I could like well enough.
> LADY BRUTE: What do you think you should dislike?
> BELINDA: My husband: a hundred to one else.
> LADY BRUTE: Oh! You wicked wretch! Sure, you don't speak as you think?

BELINDA: Yes, I do: especially if he smoked tobacco.

LADY BRUTE: Why, that, many times, takes off worse smells.

BELINDA: Then he must smell very ill indeed.

LADY BRUTE: So some men will, to keep their wives from coming
near them.

BELINDA: Then those wives should cuckold them at a distance.

Now *there's* a message the American Legacy Foundation should run with: if you keep smoking (or farting), your wife will start banging some guy who doesn't!

Chapter 35

THE DERRIERE DIVA:
FLATULENCE MEETS ELEGANCE

She's classy! She's sassy! She's gassy! She's flatomusicologist Flatulina Fontanelle Boutier, just the kind of plucky girl who turns lemons into lemonade, troubles into bubbles, and butt pops into pop music. Her attitude is a breath of air, though not necessarily fresh.

Flatulina claims to be the flatulent love child of circus clown Bubbles Boutier and rock god Nigel Tufnel from the fictional heavy metal group Spinal Tap. Following her mother's death in a balloon animal accident, young Flatulina accompanied her dad on his band's "Break Like the Wind" tour as a way of coping with her loss. But because of her chronic anxiety, she began to suffer from an extreme form of gastritis called hypergastrosplosia. That's when she donned her rose-colored glasses and white wig, and developed her sleight-of-butt magic act, she says.

But this fishy tale doesn't get really fishy until a couple of years later. As Flatulina tells it, "One late night I had a stomachache. I got up, went to the kitchen, cut some cheese, and then it hit me: train fish to sing. The rest is history." She invented flatomusicology, defined as "the study of music created by bubbles." She trained fish to mimic melodies and, with underwater recording equipment, recorded the first-ever fish choir. Adding her own explosive talents to the mix, she came up with the "effervescent sounds" of *Flatulina's Fabulous Holiday Spectacular* (2002)—a CD complete with videos—and decked the halls with bowel burps. (Visit www.flatulina.com for details on getting a copy.)

Despite all the theatrics and the odd conceit of falsetto fish harmonizing with C-flat flatulence, Flatulina's takes on Christmas standards like Tchaikovsky's "Dance of the Sugar Plum Fairy" and Leroy Anderson's "Sleigh Ride" are intricately arranged and professionally performed. Whether the farts are real or not, they sound real—and they're plentiful.

"The whole idea behind Flatulina was honestly to pay off some student loans," the poot princess confessed recently from her home in Nashville. "I'm a professional musician, and this was simply a side project for me to generate income. Sort of an intersection of my musical skills, my quirky sense of humor, my business drive, and an old childhood party trick of producing a pallet of fart sounds." She keeps her real identity secret and separate from her Flatulina alter ego because she doesn't want to lose credibility as a legit musician. "I want to be able to do other projects with my real name and not have people think, 'Where's the funny stuff?'"

Though it's considered unladylike, flatulence has always amused her. "To me, the sound of farts is way funnier than jokes about them. So I wanted to use that element in an unexpected musical setting, like Christmas songs and classical music. But I also knew that I'd need more sounds to work with besides just farts and an orchestra, so I came up with the story of the singing fish and added bubbles and kazoos. That opened up a lot more possibilities in the arrangement. When I was working on the first few songs, I was so deep in the detail work, I couldn't even tell if it was funny. But then some friends stopped by and I played it for them, and I knew I was on to something."

She wanted Flatulina to be a cartoon figure, until she realized she'd have to hire animators to bring her to life. "Ultimately, it was easier and cheaper for me to get a costume and pose for the camera."

Still, Flatulina doesn't want you to think her music is just one big fart joke. "When I do radio interviews, I tell the deejays ahead of time not to use the word fart, or else they'll start talking about farts and there's nowhere else to go. I think it's funnier to just conduct an interview and put a bunch of random fart sounds in the background."

After releasing her CD, Flatulina discovered that she had an unexpected constituency. "One thing that took me by surprise was that after I put myself on the CD cover and started doing interviews, there was this demographic of men who seemed to fall in love with Flatulina," she said. "I saw reviews on websites that said she was foxy and hot, and deejays who said she was their dream woman. I find that amusing, but I don't want to cater to any pervs out there."

She also doesn't want to be Miss Methane. "It's important to keep my project kid friendly, because kids do love it. So I've tried not to go in directions that associate me with more raunchy or sexual programs or products. That's why I've never tried getting anything to Howard Stern."

Though her first album celebrates Christmas, Flatulina points out that none of the songs have anything to do with Jesus. "It's all about sleigh rides and decking the halls. No one's feelings would ever be hurt from my CD, no racial groups offended, no innocence robbed. It's just farts set to music."

The fact that Flatulina hasn't performed live yet suggests either that she really hasn't schooled those schools of singing fish very well, or all those farts are just studio trickery that can't be duplicated onstage. But she claims to have another excuse for not taking her Flatulina persona on the road: "My mother-in-law has no idea Flatulina or this CD exist, and I want to keep it that way. She already doesn't get me."

Chapter 36

DVD, THE FART
AFICIONADO'S BEST FRIEND

In 1968, the flamboyant actor Kenneth Williams, who starred in the bawdy British *Carry On* comedies, was in the middle of a mock seduction scene with Joan Sims on the set of *Carry On . . . Up the Khyber* when he suddenly let off a couple of doozies. Miss Sims was quite offended, and as she made a big stink about it in front of the cast and crew, Williams tried to leaven the tension by remarking that Rudolph Valentino, the greatest film lover of them all, used to "blow off" in front of his leading ladies all the time.

"That may be true," Miss Sims countered, "but those were *silent* films."

It's a great riposte, but regardless of silence or sound, Williams's real-life farts never would have made it to the big screen (though an elephant's fat flatus did put an exclamation point on *Carry On . . . Up the Khyber*'s opening scene). The editor would have used a different take or simply removed the noises, and that would have been the end of it.

But nowadays, because of the DVD, nothing is wasted and tossed, not even a stray fart, which will almost certainly be picked up, because we've got sound and plenty of it, thanks to sensitive microphones and Dolby 5.1 surround sound.

The DVD—which originally meant "digital versatile disc," though "video" has more recently taken over the V—was introduced commercially in 1997 as a replacement for the VHS videotape, but movie studios immediately saw new possibilities in the shiny little platter. Like videotape, the DVD extends a film's life beyond its original theatrical run into what Hollywood calls an "aftermarket." But equally important, the DVD's enormous capacity allows the addition of all sorts of little extras not available the first time around. (In all fairness, many of these extras were first introduced on the larger laser disc, but that format never caught on with the general public.) For example, since a film has to be rated by the Motion Picture Association of America (MPAA) before major theater chains will handle it, studios usually trim objectionable content to avoid the dreaded scarlet letters—NC-17 and R—that would prevent the all-important adolescent movie fans from packing the seats. But since DVD movies don't have to be rated, producers can put all the sexy, gross, and ultraviolent stuff back in—and add a few more extras besides. According to Home Media Research, when two versions of a movie are released simultaneously on DVD, the unrated version accounts for 80 to 90 percent of sales. "People—young males, especially—want to choose what they see, they don't want censors in their lives," Home Media Research's Judith McCourt told the *Los Angeles Times* in 2005.

This repackaging sometimes provides the discerning butt-burp aficionado with not just more flatulence, but louder, more extreme flatulence, along with crepitation commentary. Which means that now, in addition to the history of Tinseltown farting (recounted in the "Gone with the Wind" chapter in *Who Cut the Cheese?*), there's an alternate DVD fart reality. For instance, take New Line Cinema's 2004 stoner comedy *Harold & Kumar Go to White Castle*. The title tidily sums up the plot: After smoking a bag of marijuana, roomies Harold (John Cho) and Kumar (Kal Penn) get a bad case of the munchies and head out to find a White Castle hamburger joint. Along the way, they stumble into several ridiculous situations. Running from a college campus cop, they duck into a ladies bathroom and hide in the middle stall. Two coed hotties in short, pleated skirts stroll in, take the stalls on either side of them, and start an unladylike commode competition by ripping a volley of wet, noisy "battle shits" at each other. It's the ultimate teenage male fantasy: young chicks who love to flaunt their farts and entertain themselves with ass gas as much as guys do. On the 2005 unrated DVD (with "Extreme Unrated" marked conspicuously on the cover), the producers not only beefed up the scene with some extra rectal rumblings, but added a bonus featurette called "The Art of the Fart," which demonstrates in vulgar detail how recording engineer Jeff Kushner captured the sound of "real" farts by hiding out with microphones in truck stop toilets. "Imagine an artist's palette, with instead of different kinds of paint it's got different farts on it," he tells director Daniel Leiner. "And you can just choose the kind you want, blend them together, and create the right feeling." Despite Kushner's comment that "women's farts are different" (implying softer, more delicate), we later see him "out in the field," trying to coax a couple of horses into blasting some real barnyard butt burners into his mic. This behind-the-scenes look at creating cinematic flatulence is, of course, bogus, and the echo-heavy shit-farts he supposedly picks up from the thunder bowls of various bathrooms sound suspiciously like an underground 1978 record on the Uranus label called "The Biggest Bowel Movement Bar None." It's likely that "The Art of the Fart" was inspired by the "Behind the Gas" mini-doc on the *Kangaroo Jack* DVD, described in chapter 6.

The recent DVD for Amblin/Warner Bros.'s *Goonies* (1985) includes Cyndi Lauper's MTV music video for "The Goonies 'R' Good Enough," which included a couple of fart sight gags.

The DVD for *Star Wars, Episode 1: The Phantom Menace* (1999) has a bonus called "The Complete Podrace Grid Sequence," an extended version of the film's opening ceremonies and podrace, including a shot of an Eopie, a hairy quadruped, farting lustily into the face of Jar Jar Binks as he detaches a pod from its rear quarters. Binks almost passes out from the odor.

On DVD, even cartoon figures are caught farting off-camera. Both Disney's traditionally drawn *Brother Bear* (2004) and Pixar's computer-animated *Toy Story* (1995) feature fart-heavy credit-roll gags, despite the fact that the films were aimed primarily at kids. Then again, maybe that was the point. Kids love farts, no matter what the adult censors at the MPAA think.

Universal's *The Nutty Professor II: The Klumps* (2000) was already a flatulence-heavy PG-13 theatrical movie, with a dream sequence in which a fart propels Eddie Murphy's title character through the air, as well as a dinner scene where a candle ignites Papa Klump's gas and blows up a restaurant. But when it came time for the DVD, the studio released an "enhanced" version called *The Nutty Professor II: The Klumps Uncensored,* with roughly two minutes added that would have upped its PG-13 rating to an R in a theater, thanks to a couple of new scenes—recognizable because of a yellow tint—with even grosser gassy humor.

But almost none of these farts are spontaneous or even genuine. Just about every gag reel and deleted scene on today's home releases are scripted and shot with the DVD market in mind. Even bloopers are usually manufactured. That's why the DVD's greatest fart bonus is probably found on *Revenge of the Pink Panther* (1978). In the original movie house version, Peter Sellers (playing Inspector Clouseau) and several gangsters get into an elevator and face the door (where the camera happens to be), staring blankly ahead as elevator riders are wont to do. Suddenly someone farts, and everybody looks uncomfortably at the ceiling or glances at someone else. But in the DVD's outtakes we see that the fart sound that director Blake Edwards used live to cue the actors was so funny that they all cracked up. And then, over the next couple of takes, it didn't matter what the fart sounded like, Sellers couldn't stop giggling and nobody else could keep a straight face.

As a great philosopher (well, maybe it was just me) once said, "One real fart is worth a thousand reel farts."

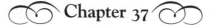

Chapter 37

NOT SO QUIET ON THE SET

Not all of Hollywood's poot play ends up on DVD. Some of it just gets picked up as gossip and blathered via the celebrity media. And why not? Everything that famous, beautiful people do is magic, even when it smells like shit.

According to an Internet Movie Database (http://imdb.com) item dated May 28, 2002, British actress Helena Bonham Carter, known for her upscale Merchant Ivory roles, farted during her sex scene with Paul Bettany on the set of *Heart of Me*. Bettany, best known as the albino monk assassin in *The Da Vinci Code*, jokingly admitted later that he was horrified—not by Helena's stinky wind, but by her claiming such proud ownership of it in front of everyone on the set. He said, "She farted on me, announced the fact to the cast and crew, and of course *I* was the one who ended up feeling embarrassed." But the episode didn't put Bettany off working with the actress in the future: "She's barking mad, keen as mustard, and funny as fuck!" he said in the way of a compliment.

TV Guide (August 21, 2005) reported that actress Holland Taylor, who plays Charlie Sheen's mother on CBS's *Two and a Half Men*, was asked during a July 20 press conference why there was so much flatulence humor on the show. "We have to have fart jokes because everyone in the cast farts constantly," said the regal actress, no stranger to on-the-set eructations, having costarred eight years earlier in Disney's 1997 fart-fest *George of the Jungle*. Costar Jon Cryer, who plays Taylor's other son, blamed it on the food. "It's a catering issue, really," he joked. They also pointed out that Angus T. Jones, Cryer's young son on the show, contracted a severe case of the giggles when he had to say, "You almost made me poop my pants." "That had him going for hours," Cryer said. "He almost pooped his pants."

Actor/comic Jack Black says he uses farting as a way of shedding his inhibitions before shooting a scene. On the road promoting *The School of Rock* in 2005, Black told Thomas Chau of Cinema Confidential (http://cinecon.com), "I don't want to say this 'cause it sounds dumb, but one time I cut a really big fart. It was really rude of me, but I thought about this thing—one time I was in this movie with Jim Carrey . . . I had a really small part in *The Cable Guy*. I remember he slam-dunked the ball in that one scene where he's playing basketball and the whole backboard shatters. . . . When we shot that scene, he was laying on the ground and they yelled, 'Action!' And then, BRRRRRRAAAAAAAAAAAAP! The loudest fart you've ever heard. They just continued with the scene as if nothing happened. Everyone just broke down laughing so hard and I remember not laughing, just going, 'There's a lesson to be learned. [Carrey] just does not give a shit what you think. That's why he's so fucking funny.' It sounds stupid that I learned a lesson from his giant fart. So [mine] was a bit of an homage to the master.'" So far, we haven't heard whether Black's later costar, King Kong, also farted to break the ice, but since there were no reports of a massive explosion or deaths by asphyxiation on the film's New Zealand set, Kong probably kept his gas to himself.

Some actors are reticent about admitting to passing wind themselves, but more than willing to talk about others. On April 30, 2003, when Rebecca Romijn-Stamos was a guest on the *Tonight Show with Jay Leno* to discuss her role as the blue-tinted, shape-shifting Mystique in *X2*, she recounted in chatty, even pointless detail the problems of sharing a costume with the girl who did her stunts.

> JAY LENO: You had a stunt double?
> REBECCA: I had a stunt double. Oh, yes, Vicki, my stunt double.
> She was my stunt double in the first [*X-Men*] and in the
> second one, because Mystique has this very unique sort of

acrobatic fighting style and they needed to find a gymnast who's as tall as I am, which are few and far between. So we found this very, very, very nice girl named Vicki, who's become a really, really good friend of mine. This is my favorite Mystique story. And I had to clear this with Vicki to tell this on your show tonight, because it's—I wish it happened to me. I'm really jealous it happened to her and not to me. When you're in this costume, obviously, everyone's gotta have their little bodily functions, you know. She came in the trailer one day and she was like, "I have to fart." [*Audience laughter.*] She goes, "I have to fart." So she farted in her costume. The back piece is like one huge prosthetic that covers your back. [The gas] ended up in a bubble right here. At the base of the piece. [*Laughter.*] Which she then had to push up her back, until it came out right here next to her shoulder.

JAY: Oh, oh! [*To the audience:*] Is she one of the guys, or what?
[*Laughter and applause.*]
REBECCA: I'm sorry.
JAY: That's a wonderful story.
REBECCA: And then she smelled it.
[*Laughter.*]

Latina actress/comedienne/lesbian Marga Gomez, in her one-woman show called *Los Big Names*, joked about her time as a cast member of the 1999 sci-fi film *Sphere*, dealing with, among other things, Dustin Hoffman's chronic flatulence. Apparently Hoffman, besides being gassy, considers farting a source of good humor. Meryl Streep once said that on the set of *Kramer vs. Kramer* (1979), Hoffman kept Justin Henry, the kid who played their son, focused by being, as she put it, "a walking whoopee cushion" of flatulence jokes.

And now we end this chapter on a somber, yet uplifting note. When Australia's renowned comedian Gordon Chater died at the age of seventy-seven in 1999, actor Warren Mitchell, who costarred with Chater in a 1981 production of *The Dresser*, recalled: "He could be so funny, and he was a naughty farter on stage—there he'd be, lying on his couch as the ham actor with this great belly—it wasn't padding—

and there'd suddenly be this loud noise. We were unable to speak for minutes." Athletic actor Rex Mossop remembered appearing in a scene with Chater in an episode of the popular 1960s TV show *My Name's McGooley, What's Yours?* "The scene was to show Chater being near-strangled in my headlock, on closeup," said Mossop. "I was to use a lot of facial expression indicating how hard I was trying. *Action!* Chater struggles valiantly for about fifteen seconds, suddenly goes limp, and then emits one of the famous Chater farts, which brings the cast and crew completely undone!"

Let him R.I.P.

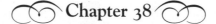

Chapter 38

LAW & ODOR:
CREPITATING INTENT

What's with those gassy gendarmes, farting felons, and scatological scofflaws?

On June 6, 2001, Reuters reported that London police were seeking a flatulent flatfoot after a family complained that he farted in their home during a drug raid and failed to apologize. "We can confirm that the department is investigating an incivility charge during the search of a home under the Misuse of Drugs act," a Scotland Yard spokesman said.

The department's letter of reprimand to the butt-blurting bobby was printed in London's *Daily Mail* newspaper: "An allegation has been received from a person in the house that one of the male officers broke wind and did not apologize to the family for his action . . . the complainant felt it was rude and unprofessional." Police did not confirm what discipline the officer might receive if found guilty of breaking wind. Perhaps a black mark in his jacket (to match the brown mark in his underwear).

Two years later, a policeman in Fullerton, California, was reprimanded for farting in a victim's face. According to the *Los Angeles Times,* here's how the crime went down. Four officers responded to a possible suicide in a trailer park. When they entered the trailer, they found a woman lying on her bed, seemingly unconscious. They knew her from previous calls as someone who drank too much, made too much noise, and often passed out. After the officers tried to wake her by shouting her name and shaking both her and the bed, one of them lowered himself inches from her face and, according to the reporter, "passed gas loudly," saying, "This ought to wake her up." He didn't realize that she was only feigning unconsciousness; hence the charge of, well, maybe it was *ass*ault with a deadly (but not so silent) weapon.

Occasionally a perp strikes back. According to the BBC News (September 7, 2001), after David Paul Grixti, a twenty-eight-year-old Australian, was fined $200 in the Werribee Magistrate Court for "letting the flatulence escape" in a public place, he appealed to County Court Judge Leslie Ross and won.

The case against Grixti was based on an incident at Werribee police station thirteen months earlier. Local officers said that he approached the counter at the station watch house and, after being asked if he needed help, "poked the rear end of his body out" and farted. Senior Constable Shane Andrew Binns testified that Grixti was staring right at him as he did it, and that his farts created a stench in the station. A second witness also told the court that the farting had been deliberate. But Judge Ross ruled that breaking wind was "quite often involuntary" and that Grixti's bending over to make the situation "a little more comfortable" was not proof of intent to pass gas. "I don't believe . . . you can turn that particular piece of human behavior on at will," the judge said.

Case dismissed.

But there are times when the miscreant does go to prison. In 1994, the *New York Daily News* reported that early on the morning of October 30, a fart pointed the finger at a "career criminal." Richard Magpiong, fifty-six, was burglarizing an upscale Fire Island home when several residents came downstairs to check out the noise they'd heard. Magpiong hid in a closet while they looked around, and he might have gone undetected if he hadn't suddenly let one go. They yanked the door open and held him (along with their noses) until the police arrived. He had forgotten the burglar's creed: when you're on a job, windows and wind should never be broken loudly.

A lawsuit by an inmate who blamed prison food for his flatulence problem was among "the looniest lawsuits of 1999," according to a legal watchdog group, Michigan Lawsuit Abuse Watch. The case lingered for so long in the public imagination that it became Exhibit A—Case No. 9650302—when the state's assistant attorney general testified before the Michigan Senate Judiciary Committee six years later, in January 2005, that frivolous prisoner lawsuits were overburdening state and federal courts.

Nineteen ninety-nine must have been a big year for flatulence-related lawsuits ("We're gonna fart like it's 1999"). Overlawyered (http://overlawyered.com) reports that in August of that year, the Massachusetts Commission Against Discrimination dismissed a Plymouth city employee's complaint that her boss had inflicted a hostile working environment on her with his constant butt crackings. She was fuming—almost as much as he was.

Going back to Michigan, the January 23, 2005, edition of *The Detroit News* reported that Washtenaw Circuit Court Judge Timothy Connors had finally gotten around to setting a court date for a case filed two years earlier, when DaimlerChrysler employees Bekele Gedion and Jose Alva sued the company for failing to control racial harassment and other offensive workplace behavior, including a May 2002 incident in which employees made farting sounds at them over the public address system.

Not even our nation's courtrooms are safe. Clark Head, who was a Calaveras County, California, criminal defense attorney in the 1980s, appealed the conviction of his client on burglary charges because the prosecuting attorney "broke wind about one hundred times" and severely distracted the jury during Head's final argument. He said the prosecutor "even lifted his leg several times." But the appeals court affirmed his client's guilt and called the prosecutor's conduct "harmless error."

On all counts, we the jury find the defendants gassy as charged!

Chapter 39

STINKING, YES! SINKING, NO!

Have you ever had one of those turds that just couldn't be flushed down the toilet? It's called a floater. And your tax dollars were spent trying to figure out what keeps it from going under.

Hint: There's a fart hiding inside.

As everyone knows, a healthy human turd is about 80 percent water. (You *did* know that, didn't you?) Constipation turds are only about 50 percent water, which means they're more compact; diarrhea, on the other hand, is 90 percent liquid. Anyway, whatever the density, the rest of a stool is made up of various ingredients, including fat, which scientists for a long time believed was the main flotation factor in turds that won't sink.

NEWS FLASH: I interrupt this chapter to bring you a special incident that actually happened to me. I was at a party at a nice home in the Hollywood hills where only the bathroom on the ground floor was available for guests. I had to pee, so I went in, shut the door, and lifted the toilet seat. Floating in the bowl was the biggest, meanest-looking turd I'd ever seen. It was one of those coiled Turdzillas whose release must have made the poopetrator feel lighter than champagne. I quickly flushed the toilet before doing anything else, hoping never to see it again. The water whooshed and swirled, giving it a couple of half-spins and breaking it into several pieces, but most of the turd, defiantly, was still there. I flushed again. Another slow counterclockwise spin, and . . . there it stayed, bobbing like a cork.

Well, I had to pee so I did my business, and then I flushed again. The yellow tint that I contributed to the water disappeared, but not the turd. Defeated, I dropped the seat back down and opened the door, hoping to scurry away anonymously, but several people, including two very pretty girls, were waiting to get inside. They greeted me warmly with smiles. I thought, should I shut the door in their faces and try to flush down that turd again or, if that didn't work, scoop it out of the bowl with something and toss it out the window? Or should I just leave and let the girls think I was the culprit? Well, like a coward, I left them to their fate. They and all their friends gave me weird looks for the rest of the evening and avoided me like, well, the type of guy who would donate a python turd to the party. In other words, a real party pooper. Even now, I feel flush just thinking about it.

Anyway, back in 1972, Dr. Michael D. Levitt, who had not yet earned his title of "King of Gas" (see chapter 18), and Dr. William C. Duane published an article in the *New England Journal of Medicine* called "Floating Stools: Flatus Versus Fat." Having first discovered that they could get small amounts of "colonic methane" gas out of a dried turd simply by slicing it open with a scalpel, the two physicians got a grant from the U.S. Public Health Service and set about to find out how much gas there was, and whether it was enough to have a pneumatic effect. After slicing several stools into small cubes, they put them in flasks containing distilled water and then applied two kinds of pressure. (Don't ask me how.) Positive pressure let them measure "critical sinking pressure" and negative pressure yielded "critical floating pressure."

The doctors' findings were almost airtight: the more fart gas that's trapped inside a turd, the harder it is to send it swirling down the crapper.

The National Institutes of Health (NIH) agrees. According to its MedlinePlus website (http://medlineplus.gov), "Stools that float are generally associated with some degree of malabsorption of nutrients or excessive flatus (gas). . . . A change in dietary habits can lead to an increase in the amount of gas produced by bacteria in the gastrointestinal tract. Similarly, acute gastrointestinal infections can result in increased gas content in the intestines due to rapid movement of food through the GI tract. One misconception is that floating stools are caused by an increase in the fat content of the stool. In fact, it is increased gas levels in the stool that make it less dense and allow it to float."

But don't worry too much if your farty, non-fatty feces keep hanging around inside the bowl. "Most causes are benign," says the NIH, "and will resolve when the infection ends or the bacteria in the GI tract adjust to the changes in your diet."

Maybe it's time to update Benjamin Franklin's old adage to "Fish and visitors—and turds—stink after three days."

Chapter 40

AN INTERPLANETARY WHIFF

When NASA and the European Space Agency landed the Huygens spacecraft on Titan, Saturn's biggest moon, on January 14, 2005, they discovered that Titan's windy surface is covered with pools of methane kept in a liquid state by the –290°F temperature and heavy atmospheric pressure. As the heat from the retro-rockets kicked up a fart cloud of enveloping methane gas, Huygens's sensors duly sniffed, analyzed, and reported the results to the Cassini mother ship orbiting overhead, as if to say, "Look what I did, Mommy."

Will NASA be sniffing Uranus next?

Chapter 41

TWO FARTS WAFT INTO A BAR . . .

What's a fart book without some fart jokes, limericks, and poems? Let's face it, you're only young once, but you can laugh at farts like an immature dimwit all your life. In *Who Cut the Cheese?* I tried to organize the most popular ones, show their variations, and give a brief explanation of the humor behind them. But this time around I'm just throwing out a few random funny bits I've picked up over the last several years.

An Irish immigrant named Mrs. Murphy has a restaurant in Ohio that's famous for its Non-Gassy Bean Casserole. That's exactly what it says on the menu. "Mrs. Murphy," many first-time customers ask, "why doesn't your bean casserole make you fart?"

"Because I use exactly 239 beans," she says in her lilting brogue.

"Just 239 beans? Why 239?"

"Well, if I used one more bean, it'd be too farty."

When a Kentucky mountain woman visits her doctor, he tells her to come back in a couple of days with a specimen. She goes home and asks her husband, "What's a specimen?"

He says, "Danged if I know. Go next door and ask Edith."

The woman goes next door and comes back in twenty minutes with her clothes torn and her face covered with cuts and bruises.

"What in the Sam Hill happened to you?" asks her husband.

"Danged if I know," she says. "I asked Edith what a specimen was and she just told me to go piss in a bottle. I told her to go fart in a jug, and then all hell broke loose."

A doctor, during his weekly visit to a nursing home, notices that one of his elderly patients, Mr. Whipkey, has begun to lean sideways in his chair. One of the nurses rushes up behind and catches him.

The doctor goes over and says, "Afternoon, Mr. Whipkey," and presses his stethoscope against the old man's sunken chest. "How are you feeling today?"

As the doctor listens to his heartbeat, Mr. Whipkey begins to lean in the other direction. Again the nurse grabs his shoulders and straightens him up.

"How do you like it here?" the doctor asks him.

"Oh, fine, Doc," says the old man, "'cept this nurse won't let me fart."

Birds of a feather
Flock together;
But birds that fart
Flock apart!
  —Mitchell Trauring

A West Virginia woman rushes her little boy down the holler to Doc LaPann's office in Osage and declares, "Oh, please, doctor, please, Wesley here just swallowed one of his daddy's .22-caliber bullets, what are we gonna do?"

Doc LaPann calmly pats Wesley on the head. "Just take him back up home, give him a spoonful of castor oil, and don't aim him at anybody."

There was a young man from Rangoon
Whose farts would make anyone swoon.
When you'd least expect 'em
They'd burst from his rectum
With the force of a raging typhoon.

While the waiter is taking orders from several well-dressed women, one of them accidentally lets an audible fart, then flashes an angry glance at the young man and snaps, "Waiter, stop that!"

"Yes, ma'am. Which way did it go?"

It was December 30, and the penniless old lady was shoplifting some supplies for her grandkids' New Year's Eve party. Suddenly the store owner on the other side of the counter shouted, "Put that bag of confetti back!"

She was so startled at being caught that she let a loud fart.

"And put the horn back, too!" said the proprietor.

There was a young lady named Carter
Who was very well known as a farter.
Her deafening reports
During various sports
Made her much in demand as a starter.

Late one night at the end of a long shift, Bob and Tim, two airline mechanics at Denver's Stapleton Airport, decide they need a stiff drink, so they spike a couple of Cokes from the soda machine with a little bit of jet fuel.

Next morning, Bob calls Tim and asks, "How you feeling?"

Tim says, "Man, I feel great. Not even a hangover. That stuff sure was smooth."

Bob says, "Well, there is one side effect. Have you farted yet?"

"No, why?"

"'Cause I'm calling from Detroit."

Overheard in an elevator:

> TEENAGER: "Excuse me, sir, did you just fart?"
> OLDER GENTLEMAN: "Did I just fart? Did I just fart?! Of course I just farted, you idiot, do you think I smell like this all the time?"

This one comes from comic Sean Morey, who does a deadly impression of 60 Minutes's TV curmudgeon Andy Rooney: "It's weird when pregnant women feel the baby kicking. They say, 'Oh my God, he's kicking, do you wanna feel it?' I always feel awkward reaching over there. Come on! It's weird to ask somebody to feel your stomach. I don't do that when I have gas. 'Oh my god, give me your hand. It won't be long now!'"

A man walks into a diner and says to the waitress, "I'll have a set of headlights and four hubcaps."

This confuses the waitress, but she writes it down and goes to check with the cook. He tells her, "That's just old short-order slang. What he wants is two eggs over easy and a stack of four pancakes. He's just giving you a hard time."

The waitress thinks, *I'll fix him,* and serves the man a bowl of beans instead.

"Hey, this ain't what I ordered," he bellows.

"Well," she says, "while you're waiting for spare parts, you might want to gas up."

There once was a gaseous young gent
Who farted wherever he went.
He visited Bel-Air
And dropped a few there
So they plugged up his ass with cement.

Writer Norman Corwin came up with this one:

A talented actor named Kane
Complained of a curious pain.
It turned out to be gas
Of a very high class
Commercially useful butane.

According to comedian George Carlin, "If there are two people in the elevator, and one of them farts, everybody knows who did it."

I sat with the duchess at tea.
It was just as I feared it would be.
Her rumblings abdominal
Were truly phenomenal
And everyone thought it was me.

Blame It on the Dog

While I sat by the duchess at tea
She asked, "Do you fart when you pee?"
I said with some wit
"Do you belch when you shit?"
And considered it one up for me.

Though the duchess was a lady of class
She had quite a bad case of gas.
She lifted one cheek
And attempted the "sneak"
And left a brown stain from her ass.

What happened to the blind skunk?
He fell in love with a fart.

What do you get if you eat onions and beans?
Tear gas.

What do you call a fart?
A turd honking for the right of way.

What did the Maxi pad say to the fart?
You are the wind beneath my wings.

Here's an insult: Your ass is so tight, when you fart only dogs can hear it.

What do you call someone who doesn't fart in public?
A *private tutor.*

Laugh and the world laughs with you; fart and they'll stop laughing.

"Darling," the husband says sheepishly to his wife. "Let's try a new position tonight."

"Good idea," she replies. "You stand in front of the sink and do the dishes, and I'll sit in front of the TV and fart."

Here's a variation of the previous joke:

A man and a woman, who are both married to other people, find themselves assigned to the same sleeping room on a transcontinental train. Though initially embarrassed about sharing a room with a stranger—he in the upper berth and she in the lower—they're both very tired and thus agree to the arrangement.

Before going to sleep, the man leans over and says, "Ma'am, I'm sorry to bother you, but it's chilly up here. Would you be willing to reach into the closet to get me a second blanket?"

"I have a better idea," she says. "Just for tonight, let's pretend we're married."

"Wow, great idea!" he exclaims, suddenly fully awake.

"Good," she replies. "Get your own fucking blanket."

After a brief silence, he lets a long, uproarious fart and says, "Good night, honey."

A young guy in a strange town walks into a dimly lit tavern to get a beer. There are only a couple of customers this early in the evening, so he doesn't realize at first glance that he's in a gay bar. After he orders a glass, one of the regulars comes over and says, "You must be new around here. Would you like to play a drinking game?"

"Sure," the guy says. "How does it go?"

"Well, it's called beer football. If you can down a glass of beer in less than ten seconds, you score six points. Then if you drop your pants and fart, you get an extra point."

The young stranger, who's proud of his farts, says, "Hell, I'm game for that."

The regular says, "I'll go first." He guzzles his beer in eight seconds, drops his trousers, and lets loose with a window rattler. "It's seven–nothing. Your turn."

The stranger lifts his glass and drinks it down in seven seconds. Then he pulls down his pants.

Suddenly the gay guy, with his trousers still around his ankles, jumps behind him. "Block that kick! Block that kick!"

While we're on the subject, what does a gay man call a fart?
A mating call.

Props are also a form of joke (just ask Gallagher or Carrot Top), and when it comes to farting, there's a huge industry out there beyond the Whoopee Cushion, the Fart Machine, and Pull My Finger Fred. The Johnson Smith Company sends out a catalog several times a year called *Things You Never Knew Existed*, stuffed with items like Realistic

Fart Spray, Fart Powder, Fart Candy, the Fart Whistle, the Farting Wall Clock, the Wacky Fart Phone ("Real phone that farts instead of rings"), the Farting Bear, the Gas Guy (a plastic figure baring his ass, whose farts are activated by a built-in motion detector), Bub L. Breezer (brother to the Gas Guy, except he blows bubbles with his ass), the Fart Detector ("It really doesn't sound an alarm, but your guests won't know that"), Fart Puddy (it makes a gloppy fart when you push your fingers into the cup), the Farting Bottle Opener, the Cheeky Farting Keychain, the Farting Salt and Pepper Shakers, and various T-shirts ("I Fart Because I'm Full Of Shit" is one of my favorites, but "Nobody Listens To Me Until I Fart" has a certain existential hook).

On the subject of farts, one last item:
They've got to come out, so why fight 'em?
You can blast them out loudly
And boast of them proudly
And if you're inclined, you can light 'em!

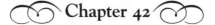

Chapter 42

FARTZILLA ATTACKS IOWA!

Ever wondered what a really big fart could do to your health, your sanity, or your wallpaper? After all, too much of anything can be deadly, so why would flatulence be any different?

To find out, let's visit Iowa, the mostly rural Midwestern state that has five resident pigs for every resident human. Thanks to the consolidation of the pork industry over the last twenty-five years, most of those pigs live in sprawling compounds instead of traditional barnyard sties, and despite the economic advantages of housing tens of thousands of them in one place for the sausage and rind-chip industry, there's one big problem. What do you do with all that runny shit? If you've ever been around a porcine pooper, you know they seem to suffer from constant diarrhea, and there's so much of it (each pig squirts eight gallons of manure a week—a lot more than you do) that modern-day managers of pig farms are forced to drain the stuff into lagoons, where it cooks in the sun, feeds legions of microbes, and stinks up the neighborhood for miles around like something out of Dante's eighth circle of hell. If you want to experience a fart writ large, this is the place. To make matters worse, among the 160 or so compounds contained in pig manure are ammonia and hydrogen sulfide, both harmful to humans. "It stinks about enough to make you sick," said one farmer, Kurt Kelsey, from the Iowa Falls area. A retired Rockwell City truck driver, Jim Kleemeier, who not long ago won $15,000 in court from a neighboring pig farmer because the odor reduced his property value, exclaimed, "It stinks to high heaven. . . . You can't hardly stand to be outside anymore!" Since the smell clings to woven materials, people have to keep their Sunday clothes stored in nearby towns, away from the pig farms, or else they'd smell in church like something Satan had dragged in. (I'll refrain from making any pew jokes here.) Among the common American expressions you *never* hear around these parts of the Hawkeye State are "I'll kiss a pig's ass" and "I'm in hog heaven."

To warn new residents about what to expect if they move into proximity of a pig farm, one county decided to print up a brochure that included a scratch-and-sniff manure odor. It was so authentic that the print shop had to be evacuated.

This hardly seems like the wholesome Iowa of *State Fair.* If Rodgers and Hammerstein were writing the 1945 Hollywood musical today, they might have tweaked their songs in slightly different directions, such as "It's a Good Night for Stinking." And in the small town of Eldon, Grant Wood would have painted his *American Gothic* Depression-era couple wearing gas masks. But those were the halcyon years when an Iowan could proudly spread his feet wide, tuck his fists into his hips, look out over the amber waves of grain, and take a deep breath of good ol' American air without being knocked on his ass.

With all that watery shit creating fartlike clouds of annoying stench, there are plenty of inventors trying to come up with moneymaking ways of turning a sow's rear into a silk purse. Among their ideas are trapping the odor by covering the lagoons with shredded tires and straw, or masking it with orange- or cherry-scented deodorizers; sterilizing the liquid with electric shock treatment; speeding up the breakdown of compounds with a super-microbe mix called Biozyme; and feeding the swine a special swill with extracts of yucca, sagebrush, and other sweeteners to make their shit less piquant. Thanks to over $500,000 in government grants, a Florida company called Global Resource Recovery built an experimental chamber that cooks manure at super-high temperatures and subjects it to heavy atmospheric pressure equal to the bottom of the ocean. The process, says a company spokesman, renders the runoff 97-percent odor free.

These days, inspectors from Iowa State University's agricultural department routinely travel around to pig farms with an instrument called the Nasal Ranger to measure the air and make sure it's getting more breathable.

The only problem now is that there may soon come a day when gassy Iowans will no longer be able to blame their own farts on the hogs next door.

Chapter 43

OLD FARTS JUST FADE AWAY

In July 2003, during the annual convention of the World Future Society in San Francisco, gerontologists and self-styled futurists discussed how long science will be able to extend the human life span. "I think we are knocking at the door of immortality," said Michael Zey, a Montclair State University professor who has written two books on the future. Dr. Donald Louria from the New Jersey Medical School in Newark claimed that advances in gene manipulation make it likely that humans will someday live far beyond their three score and ten. "Some have suggested that there is no limit and that people could live to two hundred or three hundred or five hundred years," he said.

Other scientists were skeptical, insisting that the human body isn't designed to last beyond 120 years even under the best conditions. "We are fast approaching what our bodies are capable of achieving," said Thomas Perls, leader of the New England Centenarian Study. "To get even the average person to be 100 or to get them to 180 is like trying to get a space shuttle to Pluto." Leonard Poon, the University of Georgia Gerontology Center director who had studied more than 150 centenarians, was more specific. Citing the case of a French woman named Jeanne Louise Calment, the oldest person on record when she died in 1997, he said, "At 122 she was fairly debilitated. I visited her when she was 119 in France and at that time she was pretty much blind and having very much difficulty hearing."

These were all intriguing arguments about where mankind was heading, but when the bratty news outfit Wired News (http://wired .com) reported on the conference, it flippantly headlined the story: "Experts Debate Old Fart Age Limit!"

In other words, how long can an old fart live?

But one related topic not discussed by the World Future Society was: When does somebody become an old fart?

Time was, calling some codger an old fart or an old poop (which a few hundred years ago meant a fart) or an old fretchard (another archaic word for fart) might have gotten your ass kicked, because these were considered insults. They implied that the person was no longer useful or worth much—an attitude already chiseled in stone by this country's ubiquitous advertising culture, which couldn't care less about the over-fifty demographic. It's likely that these terms came about because older people tend to release gas more often, sometimes without realizing it, because the intestine, like any other muscle, becomes less elastic and more slack with age. Also, old men sometimes lose enough of their sense of smell that they let their hygiene slip, and if the wife isn't there anymore to take care of them, they might get a little ripe. The expression has also broadened in recent years to include someone who's out of touch with what's happening in today's culture, or who clings to old ideas or ways of doing things. Even a young, stodgy person can be an old fart under that definition.

Now, with the wised-up, self-indulgent, seventy-seven-million-strong Baby Boom generation beginning to hit sixty, we're seeing a transformation of "old fart" from a pejorative into a proud self-deprecation or an endearment—a badge of honor—as long as the old farts themselves, not some young whippersnappers, are using it. Call it the mainstreaming of the Old Fart, that funny guy who has dry dreams and wet flatulence, grows hair in his ears instead of on his head, and takes all night to do what he used to do all night. He's perfect for marketing greeting cards ("Crappy birthday, you old fart!"), T-shirts and caps ("Old fart on board," "I'm with the old fart," etc.), novelty items like the Old Fart Bobble Head ("He's not just an Old Fart—he passes new ones all the time") and Old Fart Slippers (they make flatulent noises when you walk in them), and books (e.g., computer expert Aaron Rosenzweig's *Old Fart's Guide to the Macintosh* and *Old Fart's Guide to the Internet*). They've even come up with Old Fart wine (impertinent, with a heady bouquet)—which raises the question: if Old Fart wine gave you a bad case of gas, could that be considered the wrath of grapes?

It doesn't mean that old folks today are less fearful of aging, but rather that they've co-opted this particular old-fashioned term and defanged it to the point where anyone wanting to disparage a senior citizen these days is more likely to use the term "old fuck." But even though Hallmark makes light of old farts, don't expect the company to start using the word *geriatric* any time soon, which in its clinical, dead-end way is truly scary.

According to the *Wall Street Journal*, one-third of Americans will be fifty years old or older in 2009. This being the case, America is fast becoming a nation of old farts, and we might as well get used to it.

But cheer up. Like my dad used to tell me many years ago, it's better to be an old fart than a young shithead.

Chapter 44

MOBY CRACK

If you think some folks are capable of letting a whale of a fart, imagine what whales themselves can come up with. And why not? Why shouldn't the largest mammal on earth, blessed with a three-chambered stomach, blast the biggest, stinkiest farts?

Several years ago, Richard Martin, an Australian-born marine biologist who lives in Canada, spent some time, like a modern Captain Ahab, hunting down the Great White Stinky. He even put together a spiral-bound booklet called *Do Whales Fart? And Other Questions*. Admitting that nobody had been able to harpoon any hard data on leviathan flatulence, Martin extrapolated from how frequently other mammals farted, and calculated—based on the average size and weight of nine whale species and their latest population numbers—that whales around the world release forty billion gallons of gas a year. "Whales," said Martin, "have come to represent a kind of zoological *Guinness Book of World Records*: the longest, heaviest, and loudest animals on Earth are whales. I propose that whales are due yet another superlative among the animal kingdom: most flatulent."

Then, in 2003, came photographic and firsthand proof that a whale fart is indeed an awesome thing. In an August 14 news story titled "Whale Flatulence Stuns Scientists," Sydney, Australia's *Daily Telegraph* reporter Simon Benson wrote, "Unfortunately for a group of whale researchers, nature took its course right under their noses—

literally. The researchers claim this is the first photograph of a minke whale letting one go in the icy waters of Antarctica. It was taken from the bow of a research vessel."

What happened was, Nick Gales, lead research scientist in the Applied Marine Mammal Ecology Group of the Australian Antarctic Division, was on an expedition between Marguerite Bay and Palmer Station, collecting whale turds in order to find out what the whales were eating. Standing on the bow of the NB *Palmer* with the ship's captain, Joe Borkowski III, Gales was practically on top of a whale when it let loose with a wet one. As Gales later told Benson, "We got away from the bow of the ship very quickly . . . it does stink." But not before Captain Borkowski snapped a photo.

As Gales explained, "The white bits in the photo are pieces of ice-floe, the stream of pinky color behind the whale is a fecal plume—a.k.a. poo—the large circle in the water is indeed the physical eruption of the whale's flatulence." Gales walked away from the experience a wiser man. "The general rule that flatulence is worse than halitosis is certainly also true for whales," he said.

The photo was printed all around the world and showed up on the Discovery channel. You can find it on many Internet sites.

In 1970, a marine scientist named Roger Payne recorded whales sonorously calling to each other underwater, and put out a landmark album called *Songs of the Humpback Whale,* which continues to amaze new listeners. Maybe a new CD of whale flatulence would be just as tuneful, especially if it accompanied songs like "I'm Forever Blowing Bubbles."

Chapter 45

BREAKING THE WIND RECORD

How many times can one man (or one woman) fart in rapid succession?

How long can one fart last?

So far, *The Guinness Book of World Records* has been silent on the matter. It's surprising, really, considering that boys of all ages have been challenging each other for years on who can let the loudest, longest, or stinkiest fart—or the greatest number of them in one fusillade.

In *Who Cut the Cheese?* I discussed in detail what is probably the most famous flatulence-related recording, "The Crepitation Contest," recorded in Canada after World War II. It was based on accounts of legendary farting contests going back hundreds of years, including the fifteenth-century Japanese *Scroll of Fukutomi* and the eighteenth-century French booklet *Art of the Fart*. Over the past sixty years, "The Crepitation Contest"—endlessly bootlegged and even rerecorded with more outlandish characters and better sound effects—has probably sold over a million copies. The contest pits British champion Lord Windesmere against Australian upstart Paul Boomer at the Maple Leaf Auditorium, with announcer Sidney S. Brown doing the blow-by-blow. Taking turns at the farting post, each man scores points by ripping several categories of flati, including the flooper (ten points), the fudgy fart (five points), and the freep (a measely two-pointer). In the heat of the action, Lord Windesmere loses ground and, in a last-ditch effort to literally come from behind, squeezes just a little too hard and shits himself. (The same thing happened five hundred years earlier to the honorable Mr. Fukutomi.)

Since neither the modern Olympic games nor an American sports league have ever brought competitive farting out of fiction and into the real world, the job was left to that most infamous impresario of public bad taste, radio host Howard Stern.

Stern had been farting into his microphone and doing comedic crepitus bits since the early 1980s, but it wasn't until June 19, 1998, that he invited a group of farters—three guys and a girl—into the WXRK studio for his first annual crepitation contest.

Three judges—Bob, an ex-crackhead partially paralyzed by a stroke; Sal, a stockbroker who made obscene phone calls to strangers in his spare time; and Croix, a female schizophrenic rendered somewhat lucid by medication—were asked to score the farters' performances on a scale of one to ten. A Marv Albert impersonator was on hand to deliver the "color commentary." As in "The Crepitation Contest" recording, a farting pole was set up in the middle of a ring. The contestants each had a minute and a half to do their stuff. First up was a guy named Jeremy. (Stern likes to keep his wacky guests on a first-name-only basis, usually attached to an appellation that describes their talents or afflictions, such as "John the Stutterer" or, in this case, "Jeremy the Farter.") Jeremy announced that he had eaten lots of Fig Newtons to prepare himself for the big event. He cupped his hand over his ass in such a way that it sounded like a trumpet. Next up was John the Farter, who was able to use his abdominal muscles as a bellows to suck air into his bowels, just like the fabled Le Petomane. This extraordinary faculty allowed him to fart continuously for his entire minute and a half. The third contestant was a woman named Maria whose technique was swallowing lots of air ahead of time, and then forcing it through her system and out her bum vent in the form of "log-filtered farts," as she put it. Though Maria started off with some juicy snappers, toward the end she had an accident, blurted "Oops!" and instantly crossed her legs to save face. Oops, indeed. The final contestant, who called himself Chris Crap, unleashed a barrage of butt burners and, as a pièce de résistance, imitated the quacking of a duck. When the smoke cleared, Chris Crap was the winner, with three perfect scores from the judges, and Jeremy came in second. Poor Maria brought up the rear. "You have to train your ass," Mr. Crap bragged afterward, though sounding a bit deflated.

But these were simply feats of style, finesse, and fart-letting legerdemain, graded subjectively by three of Stern's "Wack Pack," one of whom was barely in the room. For this to be a true competition, Stern needed a contest with defined, measurable goals. A baseline was set two months later, on August 26, when an eleven-year-old kid came on the show, accompanied by his proud father, and cracked off 400 farts within a two-hour period, including a blistering five-minute volley of 217—a record, as far as anyone knew at the time. Now Howard Stern's private Fart Olympics were off and running.

Over the next couple of months, several challengers came on the program in hopes of besting the kid's performance, including former contestant Jeremy the Farter (who was able to squeeze off only 80 farts), Arthur Fartowski (138 in four minutes, before he ran out of gas), Dan the Farter (206), and Matt the Farter (who tied the 217 mark).

That 217-fart world record was looking pretty durable until the following summer—July 20, 1999, to be exact—when a Florida-based pianist named Kip Kolb came on the show. Kip, like the best of the farters, used his stomach muscles to suck air in and blow it back out. He started off strong with a flurry of twenty-five farts in the first thirteen seconds, then slowed down, pacing himself at one fart per second. When his time was up, he had squeezed out 225 farts—a new milestone. Then, just before going into the break, Stern asked Kip to give a parting shot. Kip answered with a juicy ten-second rumble that sounded like he may have left a few skid marks in his Fruit of the Looms.

Later that year, on October 13, 1999, when Stern held his annual F-Emmy ceremonies—a spoof of other awards programs in which he celebrates special moments from the previous year's shows—the "Best Fart Moment" award spontaneously created another contest of sorts. The winner, a guy named Travis who had farted in a girl's face, was on the phone to accept his F-Emmy, so he took the opportunity to bleat a couple of good ones. That inspired an angry Dan the Farter (nominated for an F-Emmy for accidentally crapping on the floor while tooting along with the musical theme of the show's news segment) to call in on another line and complain that *he* should have won. When Stern got them both farting together for a couple of minutes, Jeremy the Farter called in on a third line to wonder why he hadn't even been nominated for an F-Emmy. He joined the cacophony by making some noise of his own, including his specialty, the duck quack.

Since Kip lived far away in Florida, Dan the Farter became the program's go-to man whenever Stern needed somebody who could fart on cue, even though he continued to have problems with his untrustworthy sphincter. Stern would send him into the green room every now and then to act like an employee restocking the courtesy drinks in the small fridge for the show's waiting guests. Bending or squatting down to stack the bottled water inside, Dan would blissfully ease out one fart after another while the guests (who included Zsa Zsa Gabor) reacted in various ways—all captured by a hidden camera. Whenever a guest complained, Dan would act as innocent as a lamb and deny he'd done anything. Stern occasionally brought him in to fart along with musicians promoting their latest CDs. Dan also once gave an amazing display of farting in a bathtub. But the only F-Emmys Dan ever won were for soiling himself during some of his stunts.

By 2002, there was a cocky new kid on the block named Junior the Farter, an ace at rapid firing. On March 13 of that year, Junior, age twenty-two, visited the studio after bragging on the phone that he could break Kip Kolb's five-minute record from two-and-a-half years earlier. "He sucks!" Junior announced defiantly. Taking a bent-over stance in order to control his abdominals, he started blazing like a Gatling gun, firing off more than one fart per second, a pace he was able to maintain for the entire five minutes. Barely halfway through, just shy of two-and-a-half minutes, he broke Kip's record of 225, then kept on going. When the timer hit the five minute mark, Junior had loosed an amazing 464 farts. It looked like the kind of landmark that might stand the test of time, like Joe DiMaggio's fifty-six-game hitting streak or Hank Aaron's 755 home runs.

Listening that day was a young man desperate to find meaning in his life and make a name for himself. Inspired by Junior's astounding five-minute feat, he felt he could do better. His name was Will. It would take him another two years, but eventually he would be able to achieve the title "Will the Farter."

Raised by his mother in North Hollywood, California, Will relocated to Maryland after he left high school and drifted from one paycheck to another. It looked like he was going nowhere. Gambling too much, picking the wrong girlfriends, and moving in with the wrong roommates, he was a loser. Other than once winning $20,000 on a $2 lottery card, Will could never get his shit together. He was even homeless for a year, living in his car. But Will did have one special talent from his childhood. "I remember looking for something under my couch when all of a sudden a huge amount of air went straight into my ass," he says. "I discovered I could blow the air back out." When he displayed this special talent for his cousins, they laughed. "I found out my farts were actually funny. I would do stupid shit like sit on the drain cover in my bathroom and fart into it. That would rattle the pipes." His favorite place was church, where he'd lay in wait until everyone stood up and sang hymns. "Huge loud farts would leave my ass," Will recalls. "Most of the time they were covered up by the singing, but the smell was horrible—but funny." Then one day, the twenty-four-year-old hard-luck kid, obsessed with beating Junior the Farter's old five-minute record, called Howard Stern and issued a challenge. Stern invited him up to the studio a few days later, on March 18, 2004.

As soon as Will went on the air, he tried to distinguish himself from the poot pack by declaring that he was "Will the Fart Man" rather than "Will the Farter." But Stern, concerned that the appellation was too close to his own Fartman character, insisted on "Will the Farter"—and so it remained. Playing a clip from an earlier show of Junior ripping a few wet ones, Stern asked Will if he really thought he could do better than that. Will bragged that his farts were bigger and had a lot more volume, and that he once let off a single fart that lasted twenty-four seconds.

Given five minutes to challenge Junior's 464-fart record, Will hunkered down on the floor, ready to rat-a-tat-tat, as a Stern show staffer manned a timer. But first he needed to clear his "throat." Though Will, like most contestants, used outside air instead of intestinal gas, his first fart stunk up the room and raised a ruckus. But once Will got going, the odor subsided. With his ability to let more than one fart per second, they added up quickly. By two minutes he was up to 142. But then his fart flume began to flag. After four and a half minutes he was still in the 300s and beginning to fizzle. When time ran out he only had 357 farts, far short of Junior's 464. Still, Howard Stern said he was impressed with Will's sphincter control and tonal quality. So Will, in a final and desperate effort, claimed that he had enough energy left in him to set a new record for the longest fart. He took a deep breath, first at one end and then at the other, and let it go. The whining wind gust lasted only eighteen seconds. You or I would have been proud of ourselves after such a tour de force, but Will was disappointed in himself. He knew he was made of sterner stuff. He knew he had more in him. So Stern let him make one more attempt before he wrapped up the segment. Sound effects sidekick Fred Norris began playing some bombastic new age music by John Tesh to inspire Will to new heights. He took another deep breath and let it rip. Ten seconds, twenty. The fart squeaked and squealed and whimpered and sputtered. Twenty-five. Will was straining now, veins bulging and his face turning beet red. His fart tapered off into silence. The egg timer said thirty seconds. The studio went wild with congratulations. Even today, Will's half-minute performance is, as far as anyone knows, the world's record. (If you want to savor its aural magnificence for yourself, you can download it on MP3 from half a dozen sites on the Internet.)

Only moments after Will ascended Mount Olympus with his world-class fart, Junior the Farter, feeling a diminution of his own stature, called in to boast that he was going to beat Will's record when he came in the following week. Will answered him with a long fart. Junior responded with an even longer comeback. And then, as Norris played a tape of "Dueling Banjos" from the film *Deliverance,* Will and Junior's farts joined in a brotherly duet of "Dueling Bungholes."

Later that year, in November, it was Will the Farter's thirty-second flubberbubber, not Junior's 464 firecrackers, that won the F-Emmy for Best Farting Moment. Since nobody could get Will on the phone, actor William Shatner, who has his own fart history (see chapter 27), came in to accept the award (a green bust of a black, bucktoothed midget named Beetlejuice, who's a regular on the show) and remarked that the F-Emmy indeed conferred the "sweet smell of success" on Will the Farter. (See www.willthefarter.com for more of Will.)

Can the beginning of a sports franchise be far behind? Hey, if ESPN can televise the U.S. Open of Competitive Eating, with people jamming hot dogs and pies into their big mouths, why not the U.S. Cavalcade of Crepitation?

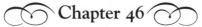

ᴄᴏ Chapter 46 ᴄᴏ

I TAWT I TAW A POOTY BUTT

H ey, poopbutt."
Or should I say "Hey, pootbutt"?

We're seeing the words *poopbutt* and *pootbutt* more often these days. A poop was originally a fart. As I discussed in *Who Cut the Cheese?* the Mother Goose nursery rhyme about Little Robin Redbreast originally read, "Niddle, noddle went his head, and poop went his hole," before the publishers cleaned the last part up to "Wiggle, waggle went his tail." According to Nathan Bailey's 1721 *An Universal Etymological English Dictionary*, the word *poop* meant "to break wind backwards softly," obviously taken from its earlier meaning, "to blow or toot, as a horn; a short blast in a hollow tube" (from the Middle English *poupe*). *Poop* would later evolve into a soft word for *shit*, both noun and verb, and be replaced in the flatulence lexicon by *poot*—now described as a soft, almost soundless fart. Hence, in one respect, *poopbutt* and *pootbutt* are very much the same.

The fact that both terms are used interchangeably, with different spellings—*poopbutt, poop butt, poop-butt,* etc.—is a result of their not being codified by lexicographers and etymologists until the terms entered more general usage in the 1980s. From all indications, both terms originated in African-American culture. Right now, *poop butt* seems to be the more popular term. Urban Dictionary (www .urbandictionary.com) defines a *poopbutt*, or *poop butt*, as "a sucker who lacks street smarts and is easily played; a mark." Among whites, it's more often used to mean "slacker" or "dipshit." As an adjective, *poopbutt* means "half-assed," "piddling," "unworthy of respect"—as in a "poopbutt town" or a "poopbutt job." Rapper Ice Cube, on the 1989 NWA album *Straight Outta Compton,* used the word in a song called "I Ain't tha 1," in which he bragged about how he exploited women before they got the chance to use him. "I ain't the one, the one that get played like a poopbutt, see, I'm from the street, so I know what's up."

In the 1988 film *Moving,* actor Ji-Tu Cumbuka told Richard Pryor, "Who you think you talkin' to? I'll stomp a mudhole in yo' ass, poopbutt!"

And going back earlier, in the early 1980s, a radio disc jockey team in Connecticut went by the name Poop Butt Perry and Bobby T.

I first heard the term about that same time when I was working with an old Los Angeles blues singer-pianist named Willie Egan, who had recorded in the 1950s. Egan used *poopbutt* so often, we named one of his recorded boogie-woogie numbers "Poopbutt Serenade."

Like Ice Cube, black mystery writer Jervey Tervalon grew up in south-central Los Angeles, but for him the word is *pootbutt* instead of *poopbutt.* In his 2006 book *The Pootbutt Survives: A Memoir of Growing Up in the Hood,* he roughly describes a "pootbutt" as a kid "who didn't gangbang" and had to keep a low profile because of it. Avoiding certain neighborhoods and streets, and staying away from house parties were all part of "the psychology of being a pootbutt who wanted to survive," he wrote in a December 2005 *Los Angeles Times* article based on his memoirs. Remembering one incident when he was confronted by a young Crip with a gun, Tervalon was able to walk away unharmed because "I was a pootbutt, not a Blood, and so not worth shooting." Early West Coast hip-hop artist King Tee used the term in his 1988 song "Payback's a Mutha": "DJ Cool Pooh, if you ever get souped up, you'll look like a poot butt, you'll ask me to stop." Five years later, two other West Coast rappers, Havoc & Prodeje, recorded "Poot Butt Gangsta" for their *Livin' in a Crime Wave* album. In 2004, Maryland novelist Van Whitfield wrote in *Dad Interrupted,* "You'll be two steps ahead of every poot-butt fool in D.C." Trying to find a regional handle on either word is fruitless.

Most likely, both *pootbutt* and *poopbutt* originally referred to a child who didn't yet have control of its bowels. Tervalon agrees. "I'm sure the meaning of *pootbutt* comes from the smell of diapers of babies who should be home being attended to by their mothers, but who are out in the streets attending to matters beyond them," he said recently.

By the time you read this, *poopbutt* or *pootbutt* may already be in your vocabulary, too. But if you read somewhere that a group of English professors is debating which word—and which spelling—is correct, you'd better drop it quick—or else everyone will know you ain't nothin' but a pootbutt poopbutt.

Chapter 47

HEY, FARTHEAD,
WHAT'S THE BIG IDEA?

Flatulence just naturally brings out the creativity in people. Kids are always coming up with ways to amuse friends or outrage their elders with butt creaks, and some adults continue the tradition into doddering old age. But those of us who are more mature or inventive look for ways to either alleviate flatulence's stinky effects, or use the gas in some productive way.

Inventors have come up with brilliant no-smell products like the Toot Trapper, an activated carbon chair cushion from UltraTech Products in Houston that actually absorbs a fart like a black hole soaks up light. You can sit there in the office and fart to your heart's content (as long as you're not making too much noise) without anybody knowing. NewTek, out of Topeka, Kansas, has a product called the Butt Muffler, a charcoal filter you strap on under your underwear. If you want your underwear itself to do the filtering, there's Under-Ease skivvies (described in more detail in chapter 8) with a built-in trap filter in back.

But some great minds wonder: why not solve the gas problem from the other end, before it actually becomes a problem, with a kind of breath sweetener that sweetens all the way through the body, like Steve Schuster's Whiff! capsules? (See chapter 28.) The first great idea in this vein, printed verbatim in *Who Cut the Cheese?* was Benjamin Franklin's 1781 proposal for a powder or pill that would make "a

Perfume of our Wind . . . and delight the Smell of those about [us]." More than two hundred years later, in the early 1990s, comedy writers for Fox TV's *In Living Color* program updated Franklin's modest proposal with a mock commercial for Flatuscents, a tablet, taken orally, that turns butt gas into pleasant aromas, including "new car." "Hey, is this a new car?" Tommy Davidson asks Jim Carrey. "No," Carrey says, "I just had a chili dog at the ball game."

In fact, comedy writers seem to be on the cutting edge of good fart ideas. NBC's *Saturday Night Live* did the *In Living Color* joke one better on January 6, 2004, with the "Magic Mouth." You insert this product into your ass, and when you fart, the air passing through it says things like, "Did you see Charlie Rose last night?"

Clearly there's a fortune to be made if the right lightbulb turns on above your head. If you need a little inspirational prodding, or you simply want to float your bright idea and get some feedback, check out a website called Halfbakery (www.halfbakery.com), which will showcase any antifart, antistink, or gas-combustion concept you're willing to send them. Though many of Halfbakery's ideas are mere whimsy, others could be tomorrow's breakthroughs. Here are some of them.

Fart lenses. A unique set of polarized lenses that let you see the light wavelength of gas as it passes from someone's ass. Slip on these stylish glasses and you'll be amazed at how many people around you are farting at any given moment. No longer is there any guesswork as to who it was who cut the cheese. Best of all, since you're able to see someone's indiscretion before the odor reaches you, you have a chance to run.

Bum tube. Because of medical conditions, many people can't control their embarrassing flatulence, but this small tubular device (no more than four or five millimeters in diameter, and maybe an inch long) could make their lives easier. It would have to have a wide mouth at one end to keep it from slipping all the way into the anus and getting lost in there like a hapless hamster. Inside the tube would be some sort of freshener. The tube would render the fart both quiet (because it provides an open, unflapping airway) and pleasant, if not odorless. These tubes could be cheap, disposable, and sold in packs like cigarettes, so that users could change them regularly.

There would also be the option to coordinate your bum tube with your favorite perfume or aftershave for increased secrecy.

Fart catheter. This small tube could be inserted into the rectum to bleed off the gases that sometimes collect there before they escape into the air. The collected flatulence can then be passed through a deodorizing charcoal air scrubber, burned in a microturbine to produce power, or pumped into a pressure cylinder for later disposal. The whole apparatus would have to be small enough to fit under clothing, like a colostomy bag. This could be handy in the office, making for more pleasant elevator rides and meetings. A compact version could even be worn to bed. Sure, your bed partner might not think it's sexy—but as soon as you remind her of that Dutch oven you gave her the other night, she'll think twice about laughing at that silly thing sticking out of your ass. A camping version could include an adapter to attach to the cookstove, thus promoting an ecologically sound cycle of gas→ heat→ tomorrow's cooked beans→ more gas.

Fart distractor (with misdirection device). How many times have you been caught trying to blame one of your farts on the family dog? Now you can get away with it, Scottie free. A combination butt plug and supersonic dog whistle, the Fart Distractor lets you fart when you feel like it without making any noise that humans can hear. At the same time, every dog within a block will come running at the first blast and get there just in time to take the blame for the stink that follows.

Breaking breaking-wind ciphers. What if the SETI program (Search for Extraterrestrial Intelligence) is looking in the wrong direction for signs of alien life? What if the aliens are actually among us, in the guise of quiet, unassuming males who furtively fart, and their passing gas is really a form of communication? Microphones and transmitters should be installed in living rooms, elevators, cubicles, and restrooms to record Unusual Flatulent Observations' audio emissions and send them on to a new Homeland Security project for scrutiny and decoding. "Brrrraaaatttt" may just translate into "Looks like rain tonight."

Belly-button pressure outlet device. Tired of releasing wind accompanied by viscous, foul-smelling liquid? Why not have a screw-in device surgically implanted in your navel to allow the release of any dangerous buildup of gas pressure in the bowels and give yourself the power to decide how, when, and where you want to have an emission. Once a surgeon has embedded a screw-type fitting within your navel, a variety of third-party attachments would be available. For example, in the dark you could turn on the gas tap and create a small illumination. It would also be handy for coal miners.

Fart louver. When you have to fart in the company of others, there's usually one safe direction to do it in (away from the people you're with) and one dangerous direction (toward the people you're with). Rather than resort to all the usual covert gestures, you could be wearing the Fart Louver: a funnel plugged in your ass, with two long tubes attached that run separately down each leg of your pants. A switch on your belt lets you choose which tube you want your fart to travel down. If you have to fart at a hoity-toity dinner function, there's no need to tilt at a conspicuous five-degree angle while you try the butt-cheek sneak. Simply choose a leg, stretch it under the table toward that snooty woman across from you, and watch in amusement as she takes the blame.

Flatulence indicator. Supposedly there are chemicals used in swimming pools that indicate when someone is peeing in the water, so why not have a chemical in the air that turns a certain color when someone expels gas. Obviously this isn't feasible outside, but a fart is rarely noticed there anyway. The most useful application is in enclosed spaces: elevators, trains, offices, etc., where it would be a simple matter of injecting the Flatulence Indicator into the air-conditioning or air ducts. Clearly everyone has an off day when they suffer from oppressive gas and try to let it slip out unnoticed, but this device would mainly be used to target serial flatulators who blatantly flaunt our clean air laws.

Fart lamp. You're finishing up your business in the toilet when suddenly you're gripped with the realization that there's still a bit of a stink in the air. No problem. You reach out to the little lamp on the wall above the toilet paper dispenser, press a button, and a flame burns for roughly ten seconds, removing the remaining methane odor before automatically shutting off.

Flatulence visualizer. Taken in pill or capsule form during meals, the Flatulence Visualizer contains a chemical that, after interacting with intestinal gas, produces colorful emissions, perhaps even cartoon-like colored bubbles. Now more than ever, you can use your farts to amuse your friends!

Sniff-O-Matic. The elevator is crowded. Suddenly somebody lets one go. Not to fear, Sniff-O-Matic is here. The millisecond it catches a whiff, the Sniff-O-Matic Silencio Model 2010, installed in the elevator at belt level, turns on the exhaust fans and pumps Scent-O-Pureness into the cramped space. Everyone breaths easy.

Many times in many ways, wise men have told us that ideas are like assholes: everybody's got one. Who knows, perhaps yours will make the world a little brighter and more piquant.

Chapter 48

MASTER STINK BLASTERS
OF THE UNIVERSE!

What's that smell?

It's a turd!

It's a plain menace to society!

No, it's a super-stinky Stink Blaster!

Whether he's Butt Breath Bob, the Silent Gasser, Rotten Egg Reggie, the Master Blaster, Porta Potty Paul, Broccoli Bill, the Stench Brothers, or any one of seventeen other three-inch-high Stink Blaster dolls, he has a soft head that, when squeezed, emits a very *distinktive* odor.

Kids love him and parents hate him—the perfect formula for the smell of success.

We've come a long way since the days of G.I. Joe.

The Stink Blasters are owned by Morrison Entertainment Group (MEG), a California-based company that specializes in developing, manufacturing, and licensing children's character toys. Prior to founding MEG fifteen years ago, CEO Joe Morrison was a marketing executive at Mattel, where he put the Masters of the Universe action figures on the map. But his Stink Blasters aren't just malodorous trolls. There's also a Stink Blasters trading card game with 144 different cards containing the twenty-four characters' histories, their arch rivals, and their best friends—each with its own Stink Rating (think Pokemon meets the Garbage Pail Kids). More recently, in 2004, Morrison launched a Stink Blasters Internet Flash game in which participants try to fart-gas the largest number of people on an elevator. The Stink Blasters figures and accessories are currently distributed in thirty-one countries, and have done especially well in Italy and Australia. Morrison hopes that in time they'll enjoy the same film success as the Masters of the Universe, though he acknowledges that the odiferous little urchins may be past their marketing prime and, in any case, might be a hard sell in Hollywood.

Though aimed ostensibly at young kids, each smelly doll is sold (at $4.99) with a detailed warning and disclaimer: "We assume no liability for any damage, suspension, expulsion, arrest, etc., that may be caused by using this product. These should not be used in any public place such as a classroom, movie theater, bank, post office, bathroom (okay, it smells already . . . but you don't have to make it worse). There are no known toxic substances contained in these units, but if you are unsure about your reaction to this product or the legality of this product in your area, DO NOT BUY IT." The stink formulas, according to one MEG executive, are about 95 percent polypropylene glycol (which carries moisture) and 5 percent oils, extracts, and food flavorings. To maintain their secrecy, the odors are put together in U.S. labs, even though the dolls are manufactured in China.

Certainly it's not young children who are playing the Stink Blasters Flash game on the Internet. It was designed by a graphics artist named "Mr. Stinkhead," who met Morrison at a toy fair in 2003 and convinced him that he should take the franchise into cyberspace. "Stink Blasters are repugnant little toys that stink really bad when you squeeze their head. . . . I was instantly inspired," says Mr. Stinkhead. Since he loved the idea of farting in elevators, he put together a game (which you can play at www.stinkblasters.com) with a choice of six characters—BO Brian, Broccoli Bill, Burpin' Buddy, Butt Breath Bob, Master Blaster, and Silent Gasser, each with its own sound effects—that ride up and down the elevator at the ten-story Smellville courthouse. Along with a character of his choice, each player gets a total of four farts to blow at his discretion. The elevator stops randomly at different floors, where passengers either get on or off, and the goal is to rack up points by gassing the greatest number of people at one time between floors. However, the player doesn't know if more passengers will get on at the next stop, or if the ones already on will get off before he has a chance to blast them, so he has to "paint the elevator" at just the right time. Secondly, there is a constantly growing fart-pressure meter that improves the point value per passenger, but if the player waits too long, his character will suffer a gas explosion and not get any points at all.

Mr. Stinkhead says that the most important elements in the design of the Stink Blasters game were the characters' farts and the expressions of the animated figures stuck in the elevator with them. "Right at the beginning of production, I decided we needed some good sound effects to get the reactions looking right. I invited over my brother to share a large ham and sausage pizza and a few beers. Microcassette recorder in hand, and trousers loosened, we were ready for action. Ironically, there was nothing. That's right, not a single blip, toot, or stepped-on duck." Ultimately, he had to rely on electronics. Hey, wait, haven't we heard this story before?

Joe Morrison says that it's no accident that all twenty-four Stink Blasters are male characters. "We decided that nobody wanted to buy a smelly little girl. Boys you expect to be grungy and stinky, but not girls."

"Stink Blasters is just good old-fashioned boys fun," Morrison told Raving Toy Maniac (http://toymania.com). "It's low-tech and nonviolent with a unique look and a great product feature that makes it something every boy will want. While our target is six- to eleven-year-old boys, we've found that Stink Blasters get a laugh from just about everyone, because most of us probably know a real-life stinker of our own."

On a deeper level, however, parents should wonder if maybe Stink Blasters, by supplying all the atmosphere and doing all the dirty work, are discouraging kids from entertaining themselves. Dammit, back in the old days, when I was a boy, we had to come up with our own stinky farts.

Chapter 49

WINDY WINNERS TAKE ALL

"T he fart game starts off around the house when you're little," Eddie Murphy said in a routine called "The Fart Game" on his 1995 *Comedian* album. "Your father introduces you to it. You'd be sitting in the house on a Saturday morning, watching cartoons, and your father make a fart and—'That wasn't me, that was your mother.' . . . And you join in, grab your little brother, sit on his head and fart. You ever do that? That's a fun game, your little brother freak out and go, 'Waaah.' And your father goes, 'It's the fart game, you'll play one day too, son.' The fart game, you . . . can walk up to your best friend while he's watching a football game and fart in his face."

All right, you're telling yourself that farting on your buddy's head sounds like loads of fun, but as you get a little older, you want something more challenging, so you move on to "fart pong" (a no-frills you-fart-I-fart-you-fart-I-fart-until-one-of-us-runs-out-of-gas game) and "bed football" (each fart is worth six points, but beware: if your opponent shits himself, he may claim that it's halftime, time to change sides). Then, when you reach adulthood, you want to move up to something sophisticated. That's why a couple of companies came up with official fart games, respectively named, surprisingly enough, FART! and FART: THE GAME.

In a 1994 episode of NBC's *Law & Order* called "Scoundrels," New York homicide detectives Mike Logan (Chris Noth) and Lenny Briscoe (Jerry Orbach) questioned a woman whose tchotchke shop included a board set called Flatulence: The Game. Logan tossed it aside with a wry shrug; one more crazy thing a Manhattan cop sees every day. But even though the game was meant to be a sight gag, *Law & Order*'s writers were probably aware that there was in fact a product called FART: THE GAME already on the market.

It's not much of a game, really. Milton Bradley doesn't have to worry about losing Monopoly sales to Baron/Scott Enterprises of Silver Springs, Maryland, a former jigsaw puzzle maker that owns FART: THE GAME. Rolling a die, you move around a rectangular board trying to pick up fart coupons. For example, one corner square says: "Farted on a terrorist. He fainted and you saved the airplane. You get five gas coupons." Other squares command you to let one fly on the fly ("The Army calls you in to test your fart for chemical warfare. PLEASE FART"). According to the instructions:

> When landing on a square that directs you to fart, you will have 2 minutes to summon up your best effort. The other players will decide what you scored on the fart meter on the gameboard. You will then be awarded the appropriate number of gas coupons. If you can't create a real fart, we have included suggestions on how to make one artificially. As a last resort we have included a whoopee cushion for those who are truly incompetent.
>
> Winning the game is done one of two ways:
> 1. Be the first person to score 25 gas coupons.
> 2. Let rip with such a powerful fart that you clear the whole room. This is known as the "coming from behind method."

Nowhere on the FART board, however, does it say, "Do not pass gas, do not collect $200."

If a farting board game with an old-fashioned Whoopee Cushion seems a little too low-tech for your liking, you can move up to FART!—billed as a "Fast 'n' Flatulent Guff Game!"—from Cheatwell Games of Sydenham, England (hence the "guff" reference that will be meaningless to you if you're an American—until you see it, along with "pphut" and "parp" and "rrrip," printed in green smoke bursts on the box. British farts apparently sound different than American farts, which never go "guff" or "parp." "Pphut," maybe.)

FART! is a card game for three to six players. There are eight farts—including the Silent But Deadly, Evil Demon, Eggy Stinker, and Teeny Weeny—with six playing cards apiece, each with a different color; plus three Gas Mask cards and four Pass the Wind cards. What paces the game is a compact disc with sound effects and three loud (but not very convincing) farts throughout. The audio "Wet Fart" means "change direction," the "Pant Explosion" means "next player picks up a two-card penalty," and the "Windy Miller" means "swap hands." I won't go into detail, except to say that you must shout "last fart" as you play your next-to-last card, and whoever gets rid of all their cards first is the winner.

Personally, it sounds a little too complicated. If I'm going to play a card game, I think I'll stick with Old Maid and simply rename it Old Fart. Whoever gets stuck with the Old Fart card at the end has to let all the other players fart on his head.

Chapter 50

BLAME IT ON THE ROBOT

In 2000, a Los Angeles–based Chinese company named Manley Toy Quest (now simply Toy Quest) launched one of the most popular items in its then twenty-five-year history of electronic games and toys: a battery-powered shiny terrier named Tekno the Robotic Puppy (not to be confused with Sony's earlier, more popular Aibo). With his "hi-tech circuitry and digital sensory input devices," Tekno doesn't just bark and play dead. "The more you teach him the smarter he gets," says his company bio.

Though he's only a virtual best friend, Tekno acts just like any other eight-week-old puppy. He loves attention. His eyes flash, his tail wags, he pants, he whines and cries. When he gets hungry, just hold his bone up to his mouth sensor (you'll hear crunching noises) and he's good for the rest of the day. When you nuzzle him against your cheek, he'll make a happy licking sound. The only things he doesn't do are fetch, scratch fleas (Toy Quest's nanotech department hasn't manufactured any yet), eat your homework, or shit on the rug. When darkness alerts his light sensors that it's time to go to sleep, his round eyes narrow into rectangular slits, and before long Tekno is snoring softly. He won't wake again until you touch or speak to him, turn on the lights, or make a loud noise.

Oh, and Tekno sometimes makes what Toy Quest calls "rude noises." You know, like farting.

And that's how Tekno put his human companion into the doghouse.

On October 24, 2003, Dave Rogerson, a thirty-one-year-old web page designer from Thorner, England, flew into Norfolk International Airport, Virginia, on his way to Charlotte, North Carolina. He was carrying Tekno, whom he'd bought as a birthday present for his American girlfriend, in one of his suitcases. But after being cooped up during the long flight across the Atlantic, the dog apparently wasn't feeling too snuggly. Just as Rogerson was going through the airport's customs area, Tekno let one go.

According to the BBC, "the toy's wind-breaking mechanism registered as a high explosive on sensitive monitoring equipment." Armed security personnel, dogged in their vigilance, grabbed Mr. Rogerson and his flatulent fido and held them in a special area for two hours. FBI agents ran forensic swabs over the pooch's metallic hindquarters for explosive residue.

"There's no humor at American check-ins," Rogerson told the BBC, "and for about twenty minutes I was quite scared. They told me it is the highest reading they had for explosives and they took it very seriously. They were very jumpy and convinced there was something explosive in the dog."

After the agents determined that Tekno wasn't a threat to national security, they returned him to Rogerson, who by now had missed his flight to Charlotte and had to reschedule another.

"Now I can laugh, but it wasn't funny at the time," he told the *Sun*, a London daily. "I kept telling them it was a toy, but they wouldn't listen. They treated me like a terrorist—they even swabbed the chocolate bars I was carrying. They didn't even apologize afterwards."

But his tootling terrier remained unchastened by the ordeal. "When you switch it on it still farts as loud as ever," said Rogerson.

Postscript

A FARTING, ER, PARTING SHOT

Tom Robbins said it best in his 1971 novel *Another Roadside Attraction*: "A sneeze travels at a peak velocity of two hundred miles per hour. A burp, more slowly; a fart, slower still. But a kiss thrown by fingers—its departure is sudden, its arrival ambiguous, and there is no source which can state with authority what speeds are reached in its flights."

With that, it's time for me to throw a parting kiss, then make like a fart and blow away!

INDEX

Index